The Book Revolution

The Book Revolution

ROBERT ESCARPIT

*Professor at the Faculty of Arts and Human Sciences
the University of Bordeaux*

GEORGE G. HARRAP & CO. LTD
London Toronto Wellington Sydney

AND

UNITED NATIONS EDUCATIONAL, SCIENTIFIC
AND CULTURAL ORGANIZATION
Paris

AND

UNESCO PUBLICATIONS CENTER
New York

First published in Great Britain 1966
by George G. Harrap & Co. Ltd
182 High Holborn, London, W.C.1 and
the United Nations Educational, Scientific
and Cultural Organization
Place de Fontenoy Paris-7ᵉ, France

Composed in Monotype Ehrhardt type and
printed by Western Printing Services Ltd, Bristol
Made in Great Britain

NOTE

The original edition of this work was published by UNESCO in 1965 with the title
La Révolution du Livre. This edition contains several minor modifications prepared
by the author

This book is affectionately dedicated to my colleagues and former colleagues at the Centre de Sociologie des Faits littéraires de Bordeaux, and especially to

MISS NICOLE ROBINE
MR JEAN BOUSSINESQ
MR HENRI MARQUIER

without whose assistance and support it could never have been planned or produced.

Foreword

THE important changes which have occurred in the publishing world over the last few decades have, as the title of this book indicates, assumed the proportions of a revolution. This revolution, like any other, has complex and varied origins, including the explosive growth of population, the spread of education and the increase in spare time which encourages the habit of reading. But, in this connection, mention should likewise be made of the astonishing advance in production and distribution techniques which have made possible the huge printings necessitated by the very increase in the number of readers. Books are undergoing a transformation and tending to become one of the main information media of our time, along with newspapers, films, radio and television.

This phenomenon was bound to engage the attention of an Organization which is required by its Constitution to promote "the free flow of ideas by word and image" and to "give the people of all countries access to the printed and published materials produced by any of them". Thus, at the end of 1964, the Unesco General Conference emphasized the importance of publications for mutual understanding and economic and social development. It likewise recognized the need to strengthen international co-operation in regard to the publishing and distribution of books, and to encourage the publication of cheap editions. Finally, it recommended that a new programme be initiated to promote the production and distribution of books in developing countries.

This study is a sequel to that by Mr R. E. Barker, Secretary of the British Publishers Association, which was published by Unesco in 1956 under the title of *Books for All*. It has been written by M. Robert Escarpit, Professor at the Faculty of Arts and Human Sciences, Bordeaux, Director of the "Centre de Sociologie des Faits littéraires", and author of several works on this subject. M. Escarpit here discusses today's publishing problems on the basis of his own, very wide, experience; the views he expresses are therefore not necessarily those of Unesco.

It is to be hoped that M. Escarpit's study, by drawing attention to the revolution in publishing, will help to ensure that the new prospects it is opening up will be turned to advantage for the greater good of mankind.

Preface

THE author would like, at the outset, to acknowledge his indebtedness to R. E. Barker, Secretary of the Publishers Association of Great Britain, who had the distinction of writing a basic handbook at a time when no serious attempt had yet been made to produce a comprehensive study of the subject. *Books for All*, published by Unesco in 1956, remains an invaluable work of reference.

Things change swiftly, however, in the world of books. Over the last decade everything has been transformed—books, readers and literature. The most revolutionary ideas have become commonplace, and in every country, no matter what its political system, men—individual researchers or scientific teams—are applying themselves to vital problems which were previously not even recognized as such. The mass circulation book—known as paperback or *livre de poche*, depending on the country—constitutes one of these problems, and perhaps the most urgent of all.

Indeed, things have changed even within the few months since the French-language edition was published. Although the study has been brought up to date as far as possible, it has been thought best not to introduce fresh but as yet unchecked statistics. The trends remain the same, and the shape of things to come can be seen as easily—or as uneasily—in the 1962 data as in the still provisional 1964 figures. If there is anything to be added with reference to the English-speaking countries, it would be to note the efforts being made by the publishing trade in the United Kingdom and in the United States to keep pace with the remarkable success achieved in creating a mass market for books.

Much of the information which appears here was assembled by the "Centre de Sociologie des Faits littéraires", which I have headed for the past five years at the Faculty of Arts and Human Sciences of the University of Bordeaux. Much has also been drawn from Unesco's documentation services, from national and international publishing and bookselling organizations and, above all, from numerous works published during recent years.

In an effort to give coherence to the various elements contained in this study, I have put forward certain provisional conclusions, and for these I assume sole responsibility. Even if they somewhat shake prevailing habits of thought, they may at least be accepted as working hypotheses. The study does not make any pretensions to be definitive; it is simply a stage in a continuing process of investigation. In any event, within a few years a fresh look at the subject will be necessary. This very transience is in itself evidence of my main thesis that the book in our era is recovering its true function as a dynamic means of communication.

R.E.

Contents

PART III: *Future Prospects*

TABLES AND DIAGRAMS

TABLES

DIAGRAMS

PART ONE

Books and the World Today

CHAPTER

I

Historical Survey

What is a book?

LIKE anything that lives, the book is not to be defined. At least, no one has yet been able to provide a complete and final definition of it, because a book is not a thing like other things. When we hold it in our hands, all we hold is the paper: the *book* is elsewhere. And yet it is in the pages as well, and the thought alone without the support of the printed words could not make a book. A book is a reading-machine, but it can never be used mechanically. A book is sold, bought, passed from hand to hand, but it cannot be treated like an ordinary commercial commodity, because it is, at once, multiple and unique, in ample supply yet precious.

It is the product of certain techniques, serving certain intentions, which may be put to certain uses. As much could be said of most of the products of human industry, but the peculiarity of the book is that the intentions, the uses and the techniques which combine to define it, far from being crystallized in the phenomenon, go well beyond it, preserving, as it were, their independence, evolving with the circumstances of history, and reacting on one another so that they mutually modify their content and lead to infinite variation not only in the book itself but in its position and its role in the life of every man and of society.

At several points in the course of this development the book has crossed dividing lines beyond which the definitions previously acceptable no longer applied, because actual mutations had taken place. One such mutation is now coming about, in this second half of the twentieth century.

The book as such seems to have appeared in its first form at the beginning of the first millennium B.C. Its appearance was probably associated with the use of various types of light, pliant supports for writing: bark, plant fibres or cloth. *Biblos* in Greek means the inner bark of certain reeds, including papyrus; *liber* in Latin means the fibrous layer beneath the outer bark of trees; *book* in English and *Buch* in German derive from the same Indo-European root as *bois* (wood) in French; *kniga* in Russian probably comes, through Turkish and Mongolian, from the Chinese *king*, which means "a classic" but which originally designated the woof of silk (1).*

Why this almost universal preoccupation with a technical point? And why this insistence upon a certain type of material? Before the discovery of papyrus and silk, were there no books? The bounds of history are continually moving farther back as older and older carved monuments are found. Excavations in the Middle East have led to the discovery of real "libraries", several thousands of years old, composed of baked clay tablets. The very roots of such words as *gramma, littera* and *scribere* go back to the time when words were recorded by scratching on some hard material, and many literary works have been handed down to us by such means. At the time when the stone-cutter alone handled writing, literatures existed, but not books; for the written record still lacked one essential quality: mobility.

Verba volant, scripta manent. Writing enabled the word to conquer time, but the book enabled it to conquer space. The pliant, lightweight supports which, thirty centuries ago, gave the book its various names opened the way to two decisive developments: first, it became possible to copy a long text rapidly and easily; and second, it became possible to transport a considerable number of copies of the text rapidly and easily to any destination.

As long as the poet was an oral story-teller, he could rely only on transmission by word of mouth to reach an audience beyond the immediate circle of his hearers. Writing enabled him to speak to posterity. Thanks to the book he can now hope, at least theoretically, to speak to all mankind. The technical revolution which created the book and made the peoples aware of it is thus closely related to the idea of diffusion.

The idea of diffusion is the clue to guide us in following the book through its successive mutations. This is most important, because it is absolutely impossible to understand twentieth-century problems in the field of literary creation, publishing, bookselling and reading if the book is to be considered only as a record, as a repository of intellectual notions or verbal patterns to be drawn on as required, or

* The notes will be found at the end of each chapter.

even as a one-way means of communication. Being a written document, a book is in fact all these things, but being a book it is something else again. Since, in a little space, it has a high density of intellectual and formal content, since it can be easily passed from hand to hand, since it can be copied and reproduced at will, the book is the simplest instrument which, from a given point, can liberate a multitude of sounds, images, feelings, ideas, facts, by opening the gates of time and space to them—and then, joined with other books, can reconcentrate those diffused data in countless other points scattered through the centuries and the continents in an infinity of combinations, each different from any other.

Details may vary greatly from case to case but the scheme is found unchanged regardless of the quality of the literary material which the book contains, regardless of the geographical, historical or social extent of the phenomenon. The book is neither more nor less than its diffusion, and for that reason its mutations are intimately related to the technical innovations that adapt it to the successive requirements of the writers whose words it records, and of the societies to which it diffuses those words.

The mutations of the book

The first stage was probably that of the *volumen*, a roll of papyrus sheets pasted together, making it possible to handle an entire work, as required by the type of literary life which existed in Athens, and later in Rome in the classical period, with its copyists' workshops (which were true publishing houses), its bookshops, and the compulsory deposit of copies in the great libraries (2).

But diffusion here was on a relatively small scale, restricted to rich amateurs, scholars in the orbit of a patron of the arts and, later, students and clerks. In the small society of the ancient city, public reading was the most usual means of publication. Shorter documents were written on wax tablets while, for everyday writings, parchment, a cruder but also less fragile and less costly material than papyrus, had been available since the third century B.C.

Just because of its cheapness and its strength, parchment was the instrument which brought about the next mutation: cut into sheets which were then stitched together, it produced the *codex*, with the page arrangement characteristic of the modern book. This arrangement is much better suited, functionally, for reference and scholarly research than was the *volumen*. It is the ideal form for legal records (*code*, incidentally, is derived from *codex*), for sacred texts and for scholarly writings. It is suited to a civilization less interested in literature than in political security, theology and the preservation of ancient learning. From the fourth century of our era, for more than a thousand years, the manuscript of bound sheets of vellum, in the hands of the clerks, was to be the universal means of preserving, communicating and disseminating thought, not only throughout the Christian world but throughout the Arab and Jewish worlds as well.

So vitally important was the book that during the Middle Ages there was no more meritorious labour than to copy or illuminate a manuscript. The transport of books from monastery to monastery, from town to town, sometimes over very great distances, was organized with care (3).

Because their artistic merits ensured their survival, we are most familiar with the beautiful illuminated manuscripts of the late Middle Ages, but there were also less costly books, especially books of hours, for daily use. As soon as they came into being, the universities organized the copying of classical texts for their students, so that a thirteenth-century scholar's textbook budget was not much greater, in proportion, than that of his successors in the twentieth century (4).

No matter how ingeniously it was organized, however, hand copying had its limits. From the fourteenth century onwards, new strata of society took up reading, which until then had been the clerks' preserve. These new readers—nobles and bourgeois, merchants and magistrates—had little use for latinizing in everyday life: they wanted technical works, it is true, but also books to entertain them, works of imagination, written in the vulgar tongue. Thus in the Romance dialects was born the "romance", the ancestor of the novel, whose popularity hastened the next, decisive mutation of the book: printing.

From the printed book to the best-seller

Printing had an immediate and spectacular effect, but it appeared only when the time was ripe—which shows that a technical innovation can prosper only if it meets a social need. Paper, which was as indispensable to the development of printing as the tyre and macadam were, later, to the development of the motor-car, had been known in China for more than a thousand years when it reached Europe in the middle of the twelfth century—and even then it was coldly received

by the authorities, who were worried about its frailty (5). Printing
from movable type took much less time—two or three years—to
cover the same ground. The times had changed, and the new conditions required that printing be discovered, invented or imported.

True, printing prospered because in Europe it encountered languages employing alphabetical script with twenty-six characters, the
form best suited for its use, but it prospered even more because it
encountered civilizations in the midst of rapid economic and cultural
development, where the diffusion of the written word was beginning
to create insuperable problems.

What was perhaps the most decisive discovery in history appeared,
prosaically enough, to the first printers simply as a convenient way
of speeding up the copying of books, improving their appearance and
reducing their cost. Everything about the typography, manufacture
and publishing of books at this time shows that the printers were
mainly concerned with commercial returns. The same concern can
be seen in the choice of the first texts printed, all of which were
likely to sell well; religious works, novels, collections of anecdotes,
technical manuals and recipe-books formed the backbone of the
catalogues of these practical businessmen (6).

The success of the operation exceeded their best hopes. Some authorities estimate the number of *incunabula*—books printed before
A.D. 1500—at 20,000,000 in a Europe whose population numbered
less than 100,000,000, most of whom were illiterate (7).

This gave the book a new dimension, and no time was lost in
exploring its possibilities. Only a few hundred copies of the first
incunabula were printed; the average printing of a book did not go
beyond 1,000 copies until the middle of the sixteenth century. In the
seventeenth century it was between 2,000 and 3,000 copies, and continued at that level until the end of the eighteenth century. It was
usually difficult to do better with hand presses, and, what is more,
the printers, who by now were distinct from the booksellers who
handled distribution, would have been afraid of cheapening their
wares by making them too common. Guild ordinances restricted
both the number of printing-presses and the size of printings. As a
result, despite a steady downward trend, book prices in Western
Europe remained at a level which made the book available to the
well-to-do burgesses, but not to the middle classes in general, let
alone to the workers. The latter, if not illiterate, had to satisfy their
needs for reading material from the more ephemeral publications to

be found in the pedlar's pack: broadsheets, ballads and almanacs (8).

It can therefore be said that the printed book, which was the support and vehicle of the great European literature of the sixteenth, seventeenth and eighteenth centuries, took it only to a very small circle of society.

In the eighteenth century, England was the least illiterate country in Europe, and the country in which publishing was the most prosperous, but even the most popular books—*Pamela* or *Joseph Andrews*—never had a sale of more than a few thousand copies (9). In France, printings were decidedly smaller, and though Voltaire's witticism—fifty readers for a serious book and five hundred for an entertaining one—was surely an exaggeration, the fact remains that the readers of books represented a small aristocracy of written culture, or of "literature", as it was then called.

It was an international aristocracy. The absence of any kind of copyright agreement gave a stimulus to piracy in publishing which was morally questionable but culturally beneficial. American publishing, for instance, developed magnificently, after the United States became independent, by establishing itself as a parasite upon the British publishing trade. Owing to their mercantile traditions or their political situation, such cities as Amsterdam and Lyons were, for centuries, international centres of diffusion for the reading public. The *Divine Comedy* took more than four centuries to make its way throughout Europe; twenty years were enough for *Don Quixote*, and five for *Werther*. Five or six major languages shared the literary universe; never has the sense of a world community of the literati been keener than during the eighteenth century.

But this aristocratic cosmopolitanism was directly threatened; the book had long been working up to a fourth mutation, mechanization, which was to destroy it. The premonitory signs were visible from the days of the Encyclopaedists on. As in the fifteenth century, new social strata, including the lower middle classes, took up reading and demanded books of a system which had not been designed for them, which by definition excluded them. This new need for reading matter was one of the causes of the development of the press, whose circulation figures were still, however, very small.

Faced with a developing market, printing and bookselling underwent a major change, as nascent capitalist industry took charge of the book. The publisher appeared as the responsible entrepreneur relegating the printer and bookseller to a minor role. As a side effect, the literary profession began to organize: until then literature had been left to the rich amateur or relied on the support of the art patron, but now the writer began to claim a livelihood from his works. From Dr Johnson to Diderot, men of letters raised the question of copyright and literary property.

In the last third of the eighteenth century, trends of thought which, though at variance with one another, all converged in the direction of spreading books among what was then called "the people"—Methodism in England, Encyclopaedism and later the revolutionary spirit in France, and, to a lesser extent, *Aufklärung* in Germany—suddenly made the need for reading matter an urgent problem.

Then, in a few years—between 1800 and 1820—a series of inventions revolutionized printing techniques: the metal press, the foot-operated cylinder press, the mechanical steam-press. Before the end of Napoleon's reign, more sheets could be printed in an hour than had been possible in a day fifteen years earlier. The period of large printings could begin.

It began in Britain, for most of the improvements in printing were of British origin. Walter Scott's novels heralded this development, but it really opened with Byron's well-known experience in 1814, when 10,000 copies of *The Corsair* were sold on the day of publication. The wave reached France about 1830 (10), together with the heavy-duty press, and by 1848 it had swept over the rest of Europe and America.

This change in scale produced far-reaching effects. First of all, the writer lost contact with the vast majority of his readers: only the "cultured" stratum of the population continued to participate, either directly or through the critics, in the formation of influential literary opinion, while the anonymous multitude of other readers now figured in the mythology of letters only as a boundless sea into whose waves the poet tossed at random the bottle bearing his message (11).

But it was no longer possible to ignore the existence of the mass of readers who thenceforth were to support the book and make it an economic proposition. Just as the fourteenth- and fifteenth-century bourgeois had made the clerkly Latin book give place to the use of the vulgar tongue, so the new readers of the nineteenth century made the cosmopolitan book of the literati give place to the use of national languages. Large printings thus both required and facilitated the splintering of literary languages, leading to independent national literatures. As nationalism awakened, the book kept step with the times.

And it kept step with the times in the awakening of class consciousness as well. One after another, the circulating library, the serial novel and the public library spread the book ever more widely among the social strata which the progress of education had opened to reading. In the revolutionary thinking of 1848, the book became a basic symbol. It was realized that the way to freedom lies through cultural conquest. As was to be expected in Britain and in the United States the popular book had a strong puritanical bias, and the stress lay more on its moral role than on its revolutionary value. Its efficiency as a social determinant was nevertheless very great, especially in the United States where, as Richard D. Altick phrases it, "the American author had learned more quickly than his English cousin how to write for a democratic audience" (12). The pirate-market having reversed its pre-Dickensian East–West trend, the American book was read all through the English-speaking world, including Britain and its colonies. By mid-century *Uncle Tom's Cabin* sold a million and a half copies in one year and played a part in the building of a progressive opinion in Anglo-Saxon countries comparable to that of *Les Misérables* ten years later in France.

But the first signs of a new, fifth, mutation of the book were appearing in Britain, where the inevitable consequences of capitalist industrialization developed earlier than elsewhere. While the newly-published book was already being sold at the price of ten shillings and sixpence (half a guinea, the luxury trade's status symbol), which was to remain current up to World War II, from 1885 onwards popular reprints of good books began to appear, selling at about sixpence and in printings of tens of thousands of copies. By the end of the century, abridged novels and poems were being sold for a penny, and from 1896 on, one publisher was even to offer penny editions of unabridged texts by Goldsmith, Poe, Scott, Dickens, Dumas, Eugène Sue and Mérimée (13).

But it was still too early for such undertakings. In a society where there was no internal mobility, the "masses" interested in this kind of reading matter were still only a privileged minority. Although Britain was rather ahead of the rest of the world in this respect, because of the rapid growth of its urban centures, the majority of the population of the other civilized countries still depended for their reading material on the bookstall and the pedlar: mutilated editions of old classics, sentimental novels, folk-tales, joke-books, ballads, almanacs, etc. (14). In some parts of the world this situation was to last until after the Great War, and even until the second half of the twentieth century.

Mass communication

But even before the turn of the century, the first of the mass-communication media had appeared, to some extent replacing the pedlar in many places throughout the world. By 1900, the popular newspaper, born of the cheap press of the 1830's, had passed the figure of a million copies. Half a century later, the British press was breaking all circulation records with the never-equalled figure of 600 copies a day per thousand inhabitants. Behind the United Kingdom, in the 400-copies category, came the Scandinavian countries, Australia and Luxembourg; New Zealand, the United States and Belgium were in the 300-copies category, while in the 100-copies and 200-copies categories came the main body of the twenty or so economically and technically developed nations which, to all intents and purposes, shared among them the rest of the newsprint consumed throughout the world.

The peak was reached about 1955. Since that time, while the newspaper has continued to develop (although at a slower rate) in those countries which had a cultural lag to make good, elsewhere it is dropping back in the face of keen competition from films, radio and television (15).

These new mass-communication media have possibilities which the newspaper cannot share. They are suitable not only for the circulation of information, but also for artistic expression. True, the nineteenth-century newspaper attempted to second the book in respect of its literary function, but the serial novel has never had a good press among the "cultured class". Even when it is of good quality, it is incomparably less efficacious than a film, a radio broadcast or a television programme.

From the end of the Great War, and with no interruption other than the five years of World War II, the audio-visual mass-communication media have distributed ever-increasing quantities of information and artistic material (both, it is true, varying greatly in quality) to sectors of society which had previously been totally neglected culturally. In the extreme case, television can bring the highest manifestations of art right into homes in which illiteracy, ignorance and poverty have barred the door to the book.

Besides their virtuosity and their omnipresence, these mass-communication media have two advantages over the book: their cost is relatively low and their "consumption" is agreeable. A fine book, on the other hand, is expensive, and a cheap one, with its dull cover, greyish paper and cramped printing, is horribly ugly and depressing. For this reason the cinema, radio and television exercise both an economic and an aesthetic pressure upon the book. When, for the price of one hour's work, it is possible to go to any neighbourhood cinema and spend two hours watching a pleasant story in elegant, comfortable surroundings, why should anyone spend three or four hours' wages, or even more, to read the same story in a book which becomes steadily less prepossessing as its cost decreases?

Of all these considerations, that of beauty is perhaps the most important. Since World War II, the use of synthetic plastics and the development of industrial design have, generally speaking, freed the outward everyday life of the common man from ugliness. In the commercial field, this evolution had begun before the War, with the one-price store, a beautified version of the Anglo-American Woolworth's. Suddenly finding himself served by shop-girls with well-kept hands and hair, in a brightly-lit shop, perhaps to the strains of soft music, gave the average consumer a strange sense of unreality. In many countries, 1935 was the year of the "chain store", during which a certain kind of beauty came into community life as a sort of public service. It may perhaps be of interest that the Moscow "metro", whose gilt and rococo, in a different social structure, fulfilled the same function of beautifying daily life, also dates from 1935. At about the same time in the mid-thirties Raymond Loewy began popularizing the theories on industrial design which he embodied in his 1937 book, *The Locomotive, Its Aesthetics*, and developed later in his famous work *Never Let Well Enough Alone*.

And 1935 was also the year in which, in England, Sir Allen Lane founded Penguin Books. The early Penguins may not have been objects of great beauty, but the red-and-white jackets of these sixpenny paperbacks were unusually cheerful-looking for books of that class. In Germany, the old Tauchnitz (16) editions were soon obliged to modernize themselves to keep up with their young competitor, and to exchange their grim typographical covers for softly-tinted jackets, with a different colour for each type of work.

The Penguin did not set out to be a book for the masses. Somewhat snobbishly, those in charge of it persisted for a long while in disclaiming this role; perhaps in fact they did not intend to play it (17). But man proposes and history disposes. Once again, a mutation had occurred at exactly the right time, the appearance of the Penguins coinciding with a concatenation of circumstances favourable to the book for the masses. A few years earlier, in France, experiments such as those of Fayard or Ferenczi, carried out in a similar spirit and probably under better financial conditions, had not yielded the hoped-for results. J. Ferenczi's *Livre Moderne Illustré* series, which reprinted the best-sellers of Colette, Mauriac and Giono, was already selling at 3.50 francs—about a shilling—when the Penguins appeared; it managed to survive somehow, but only at the price of abandoning its ideas of popularization.

The Penguin series, on the contrary, prospered, and developed in a direction which the founder had perhaps not foreseen. In any case, whether deliberately or not, by launching his venture at the precise moment when the times were ripe for it, Sir Allen Lane opened the door to the mass-circulation book.

So true is this that Penguin Books are now partly financing at the University of Birmingham the Centre for Contemporary Cultural Studies, which is working under the supervision of Professor Hoggart on the problems of the ordinary man's reading. Throughout the world—in France, Germany, Belgium, the United States, Japan and the socialist countries—these problems are of the greatest interest not only to publishers and booksellers (which is not surprising), but also to sociologists studying questions of culture and the use of leisure and, even more important, to specialists in literary history and criticism. Therein, in the second half of the twentieth century, lies the new significance of the book.

The mutation occurred rapidly, under the pressure of powerful acceleration factors, of which the War, the establishment of socialist régimes in many book-producing nations, and decolonization and its cultural consequences, were the most important.

The need to furnish abundant cheap reading matter for millions of American soldiers scattered throughout the world was probably what caused the American publisher to become seriously interested in the paperback. Whatever the ideological orientation of a country, the desire to make its national views known abroad stimulated large printings and low prices. Overseas cultural centres of the major powers distributed their books in hundreds of thousands of copies. And in the countries where educational advancement was outstripping economic development, only the book for the masses could meet the demand created by the new reading public.

Thus was born the new book which, since 1950, has practically conquered the world—even France, for years set in the firm conviction that, so far as the paper-bound book was concerned, she had nothing to learn from anyone.

The paperback is printed on ordinary, but agreeable, paper, strongly bound in a coloured jacket which is very often illustrated. It is never printed in less than some tens of thousands of copies, and it is seldom sold at more than the equivalent of an hour's wages per volume. It is wide-ranging in its choice of titles: it reprints best-sellers but also publishes original work; it includes the classics, new novels, technical handbooks, scientific works and even reference books, dictionaries and guides. Its intellectual mobility is enormous: while in 1961 it accounted for 14% of the total output of books in the United States, in 1962 it accounted for 31%, and the ratio keeps increasing. It accounts for 25% of books on biography, history, religion, science and technology, for 30% of books on art, business, education, general works, sociology and economics, language, law, medicine and philosophy, and for 46% of all fiction titles (18) (see also Table IX). In 1964 there were 30,700 titles available in paperbacks in the United States out of an estimated total of 120,000.

As early as 1960, an exhibition sponsored by the National Book League in London showed 1,000 paperbacks in thirty languages, coming from countries as diverse as Canada, France, the Federal Republic of Germany, Eastern Germany, India, Indonesia, Iran, the Netherlands, Pakistan, Sweden, the Union of Soviet Socialist Republics, the United Kingdom and the United States of America (19). But this was only a sample, and a few months later it was outdated. A revolution was in progress.

NOTES

(1) One important exception, however, is that of the Semitic languages, in which the root *ktb*, meaning *book*, seems quite unrelated to the material of which the book is made.

(2) For books in ancient times, see the nineteenth-century study by Th. Birt, *Das antike Buchwesen*, 1882, or the standard manual by S. Dahl, *Histoire du livre de l'antiquité à nos jours*, 1933.

(3) *The Mélanges d'histoire économique et sociale* offered as a tribute to Professor Antony Babel, Geneva, 1963, contain (pp. 96–127) an interesting article by M. Stelling Michaud on the international transport of Bolognese legal manuscripts from 1265 to 1320.

(4) The machinery for the publication of university texts is described in the Introduction (pp. 9–13) to the book by L. Febvre and Henri-Jean Martin, *L'Apparition du livre*, Paris, 1958. Authentic, reliable manuscripts were hired out, under University guarantee, by the 'stationarii' or sworn university booksellers, to students desiring to copy them, or to professional copyists under contract.

(5) Italy began to import paper brought from the Orient by the Arabs in the twelfth century. Paper manufacture in Italy began early in the fourteenth century, but even in the thirteenth century, despite its prohibition by certain chancelleries, paper was already currently used in France and Switzerland.

(6) On the whole of this period of the history of the book, see A. Flocon, *L'Univers des livres*, Paris, 1961, especially Part III: *Les livres imprimés anciens*.

(7) The perhaps somewhat optimistic estimate of L. Febvre and H.-J. Martin, *op. cit.*, p. 377.

(8) On this question, see David T. Pottinger, *The French Book-trade in the Ancien Régime, 1500–1791*, Harvard, 1958.

(9) According to Richard D. Altick, *The English Common Reader*, Chicago, 1957, pp. 49–50, the printings of these 'best-sellers' never exceeded 4,000 copies, and the average printing was 500 or 1,000. If it was successful, a book had between three and five printings.

(10) To be precise, in 1836, with Emile de Girardin's *La Presse*. In one year, subscriptions to Paris newspapers rose from 70,000 to 200,000 (E. Boivin, *Histoire du journalisme*, Paris, 1949). In the literary field, the effects of large printings were not felt until a little later, between 1840 and 1848.

(11) This is certainly one of the origins of the romantic myth represented by Alfred de Vigny's *La Bouteille à la mer*.

(12) Richard D. Altick, *op. cit.*, p. 301.

(13) George Newnes' Penny Library of Famous Books. See R. D. Altick, *op. cit.*, pp. 314–15.

(14) On the position in France in the mid-nineteenth century, see the invaluable, because unique, work of Charles Nisard, *Histoire des livres populaires ou de la littérature de colportage*, Paris, 1964.

(15) In 1962, printings of British newspapers dropped to 506 per 1,000 inhabitants, Norway and Denmark were at about 350, while Sweden held firm at 462 and Luxembourg at 445. Among the increases, Japan reached 416 (as against 224 in 1952), and New Zealand climbed slightly, from 365 to 406.

(16) Christian Bernhard Tauchnitz, the nephew of a Leipzig publisher, founded his famous 'Collection of British and American Authors' in 1841; in 100 years, the collection published nearly 6,000 titles. For this story and the history of paperbacks in general, see Part I of Frank L. Schick, *The Paperbound Book in America*, New York, 1958.

(17) A 1964 Penguin Books prospectus states, with characteristic smugness, "They are not a product for the masses. Eleven million Penguins sold in the United Kingdom in one year represent only one Penguin bought by one Englishman out of five. The Penguins are made for a (relatively large) minority, a select minority."

(18) *Publishers' Weekly* (Philadelphia), vol. 183, No. 3, 21 January 1963, pp. 42–43.

(19) See the article by Desmond Flower, *A Revolution in Publishing*, in *The Times* Supplement on Paperbacks, 19 May 1960, and the article by J. E. Morpurgo, *Paperbacks Across Frontiers*, in *The Library Journal* (New York), 15 January 1961.

The Functions of the Book

A composite art

LITERATURE is a composite art. The letter, which is its specific means of expression, and which has given it its name, is both an object and a sign. As an object, it has a *form* perceived, interpreted and appreciated according to a system of plastic values; as a sign, it has a *content* perceived, interpreted and appreciated according to a system of semantic values which does not coincide with the system of plastic values.

In fact, the situation is still more complex. The letter as an object is never found in isolation: it forms part of the letterpress, which itself is only one element of the artistic whole, comprising page design, printing, illustration, binding—in short, the objective beauty of the book. And if the book is to be taken as an object of art whose text (considered as a material thing) is only one of its elements, it must be seen in the context of the network of social conditions governing the distribution of art objects: trade, investment, fetishism, conspicuous consumption, pursuit of the status symbol, etc.

On the other hand, the content of the letter as a sign is ambiguous and manifold. Combined with other letters to form words, which themselves are combined with other words to form sentences, it finally contributes to the transmission, at various levels, of messages which may be rational, practical or emotional as the case may be, but which are always intellectual. As an element of thought which is, as it were, "frozen" in writing, but which can be reactivated by the act of reading at any time, in any place, the letter is an "information tool". But at the same time, taken alone or in its context, it is the visible representation of a sound. In the last analysis, to write a word is to pronounce it by delayed action and by proxy. Reading reactivates the sound content as well as the intellectual content, but the two reactivations do not necessarily coincide or coexist. The letter as a "delayed speech tool" can very well be separated from the letter as an "information tool".

It follows that the book, besides being an art object, is both a means of acoustic expression (since the sounds can be combined without meaning, like music) and a means of intellectual communication (since the meaning can be perceived independently of the original sound scheme, as occurs when a translation is read).

Many other ambiguities could be pointed out, but these three independent, if not always divergent, lines of significance suffice to show why it is impossible to apply to literature the same categories and aesthetic concepts as are applied to the other arts. To the extent that the literary act is an act of communication by means of the book, literature in the broad sense of the term both assumes the existence of the book and supplies the reason for its existence. It therefore shares the book's indefiniteness and its ambiguities. In this domain, definitions are elusive and criteria imprecise.

The literary art can recover its coherence and aesthetic rigour and be "purified", if it is set the object of seeking and maintaining a difficult balance between graphic form, melody of language and intellectual meaning. It is precisely in this that the traditional literary art of China consists and, in general, the literary art of the Far East, so far as it uses Chinese ideograms. These ideograms embody at one and the same time, form, music and thought. The whole art of the poet consists in reconciling their different natures, so that, in this sense, the ancient Chinese book may be said to be the model for all literature. The Middle Ages in Europe, with their illuminated manuscripts and their love of plays on words, riddles and verbal symbolism, had the same aesthetic idea, but it was much more difficult to achieve it with tools as abstract as syllabic or alphabetical scripts and as pitilessly rational as the analytical languages.

On the other hand, the trouble with any balance is that it is incompatible with movement. And, as we have seen, the book has never stopped moving since it first appeared. The balance attained at a given moment between its various scales of values is gradually destroyed by the pressure of ever-changing social, economic and technical conditions. Once petrified by success in the mould of one style, one idiom, one form of presentation, price or means of distribution, the book can no longer, without deteriorating and decaying, serve as a means of communication between rising generations of writers who call upon it to express what it cannot say, and new classes of readers whose intellectual aspirations and material requirements it cannot satisfy. At that point, as degeneration sets in, a mutation takes place and the balance is restored. At the turn of the century, as we have seen, having failed to adapt itself to the needs of mass culture, the book was ugly or expensive, but never both cheap and pleasant to look at. Similarly, with very few—though honourable— exceptions, the books available to the reader of limited means were hardly ever both well-written and interesting. The paperback mutation, which began in 1935, enabled the modern book to take its place in a mass civilization, while securing a new balance between concern for a certain graphic beauty suited to prevailing economic conditions, for a wider significance and a more accessible idiom.

But this balance is far from being entirely and universally established. Despite the spectacular success of the mutation in some countries, in many more it has hardly even begun. No one knows whether it will succeed in the years between now and the end of the twentieth century.

In twentieth-century societies, whether highly developed or not, the book's vulnerability is increased as it is called upon to perform a variety of specialized functions which throw it off balance and change its nature. The book as a thing and the functional book are the most characteristic of these specializations.

The book as a thing

Take a young couple in a middle-level social and professional category, such as that of skilled craftsmen, small businessmen or junior executive grades. Suppose that each of them is a regular reader, getting through, in addition to newspapers and magazines, one book a week (1). Taking into account differences in taste, it could be assumed that sixty to seventy books come into the home every year. Such readers will probably belong to a lending library, but will spend considerably more on books than the £13 a year which is the average for their category. It can be assumed that they will buy at least twenty to twenty-five books a year, perhaps more if in cheap editions. Allowing for losses, at the end of ten years they will have a library of about 200 volumes, a figure compatible with the small modern house or flat, since it represents roughly what four three-foot shelves will hold (2). If our young couple keep up their reading rate—and after a slight drop at about the age of thirty, the likelihood is that the rate will increase—their library will continue to expand, as furniture-movers well know! It is then easy to calculate that, if all the books in this collection have an equal probability of being re-read, each of them can be re-read by its owners, at best, only once every twenty years. In point of fact, there are some books which are re-read—at varying intervals, of course—fairly regularly, and they reduce the chances of the others to that extent. Historical selection, which causes 80% of literary production to be forgotten within a year and 99% in twenty years (3), while it operates less harshly in a private library than in a bookshop, because the purchase of a book "to keep" is an act of selection in itself, still comes into play.

All this goes to prove that, of the enormous quantity of books standing on private bookshelves, scarcely any are being used, or will ever be used, for reading again. The question then arises, what *are* they being used for? If they are no longer "reading-machines", what usefulness have they, and what motives induce their owners to buy them?

Generally speaking, the book as a thing can have three uses, which are never found in isolation but which for ever overlap and combine. It may be an investment, a decorative item or what is now called a status symbol—the sign that its owner belongs to a certain social category. Even the functional library of the college professor or professional man is influenced by these extra-literary considerations.

The book as an investment is disappearing, at least from the commercial publishing and bookselling circuits. The bibliophile is most often a collector of old books. Special, non-commercial editions on *de luxe* papers are becoming more and more rare: literary production has become much too abundant, and historical selection much too harsh, to support this kind of activity. A fine edition of a forgotten book is a dead weight.

The book as a decorative item still survives to a certain extent: it has indeed become an essential accessory for the interior decorator who wants to create a "cosy" atmosphere for the living-room. But this use, too, is declining as reading becomes more common. The book capacity of the modern apartment is limited. Taking into account the rest of the furniture and a reasonable amount of decoration, an ordinary two-room flat (living-room, bedroom, kitchen and bath) can hardly hold more than two or three hundred volumes. If the mobility of this meagre stock must be sacrificed to the requirements of the decorator (for nothing is less beautiful or more untidy than a library in use), reading stands little chance. More and more often the book is regarded as an "expendable" item, and the aesthetic need that the paperback seeks to satisfy is by its very nature ephemeral.

The status symbol is still very much alive in some countries, either because the general run of their populations have only recently become literate (when the book recovers the almost religious significance that it had among the common people of Western Europe during the nineteenth century), or, on the contrary, because their social structure includes groups with stereotyped reactions, such as the middle-classes in the United States. In this latter case, incidentally, it is no longer a question of expensive books with artistic bindings and typography, really symbolizing something, but of mass-produced volumes with a spurious appearance of luxury, like those with which certain international book clubs (in fact, American in origin) are now flooding the world's markets.

This, of course, is only one aspect of the 'club' book which, while it has had only slight success in such countries as France, relatively uninfluenced by the status symbol idea, has represented up to one fifth of the total sales of the book trade in the United States and the Federal Republic of Germany (4). As a French article on this type of publishing stated as early as 1956, "The interest aroused by the birth of the club book reflects the survival of the desire for well-produced, bound books among cultivated readers who appreciated beautiful books but who, because of successive currency devaluations and the constant decrease in their purchasing power, combined with the high cost of hand binding, have not always been able to build up a personally chosen library." (5)

This is, in fact, in our levelled society, one of the ultimate fates of the book as a thing. But it would be unfair to regard it only as a debasement. Technical progress in paper manufacture, colour reproduction and the use of plastics, among other things, has made it possible to add considerably to the book's merits as an object, without thereby reducing its value in use.

A particularly interesting example is that of books of the type of the *Pléiade* series in France or the *Aguilar* series in Spain. Using high-quality Bible paper and leather binding, these publishers produce books which have an investment value and are decorative, but which at the same time provide, in a pleasant form functionally suited for daily use, reading matter whose price, considering the content of the volumes, is no higher than that of the matter supplied in ordinary editions.

It may be added that the very beauty of the modern book sometimes gives it a quasi-literary aesthetic value even when it is deliberately functional. This applies particularly to school-books in countries where the high standard of the teaching methods in general use more or less rules out any competition as regards the functional value of the book and publishers can compete only as regards the book's merits as an object. The French school-book in the second half of the twentieth century is often a true art object, but it is maintaining and even increasing its functional efficiency as a teaching aid. And above and beyond that efficiency, it is becoming once more a literary reading instrument since, as many booksellers testify, certain adult readers buy it for just that purpose.

This, however, is an extreme case from which no generalization can be drawn. The school-book remains, in any case, the perfect example of the book as a tool, the functional book.

The functional book

The idea of the functional book is more easily apprehended than that of the book as a thing. Some books claim to be functional and their utilitarian purpose is unequivocal. Of the ten classes recognized by the Dewey decimal classification, four are entirely functional (Social Sciences, Language, Pure Science and Technology) and five are partly so (General Works, Philosophy, Religion, The Arts, and History-Geography).

Quantitatively speaking, the functional book holds first place in the world book trade: about 75% of the titles published annually, and about the same percentage of the total number of copies printed, are functional books.

This statement, however, should be taken with some caution, as the criteria of the decimal classification system are extremely imprecise. If all books other than those in Class 8 (Literature) are taken to be more or less functional, it is possible to gain an approximate idea of the situation in each country, but it must be remembered that Class 8 sometimes includes functional books as well. In France and the Netherlands, for example, not only criticism and books on literary history, including school and university textbooks, but even works from Class 4 (Language) are usually placed in Class 8! The table opposite shows very approximately the movement in the

actual production of functional books (by number of titles) as a percentage of total production, for the years 1938 (the last complete
year before World War II), 1952 and 1962.

TABLE I

Evolution of the Percentage of Functional Books: 1938, 1952, 1962

COUNTRY	*1938*	*1952*	*1962*
United Kingdom	55	65	65
United States	60	55	50
France	70	65	60
U.S.S.R.	75	70	85
Federal Republic of Germany	75	70	75
Eastern Germany		75	80
Italy	80	70	65
Japan	?	75	75
Netherlands	?	50	70

Despite its lack of precision, this table furnishes some useful
information:

1. Over a period of twenty-five years, the situation has changed
less than might have been expected.

2. Industrially "young" countries in the process of active economic development (U.S.S.R. and Japan certainly) are increasing their
output of functional books; it can easily be ascertained, incidentally,
that emphasis has been on the social and applied sciences.

3. The long-industrialized Western countries are relatively stable,
but with some tendency to reduce their production of functional
books.

4. The case of the Netherlands should be considered apart, because during the last few years this country has resumed its traditional role as a producer of scholarly works for the world market.

Among all the functional books, we have most information about
school-books. This category is also the most important, since with
the progress of public education throughout the world, the school-
book has become an essential commodity in every country.

In France it accounts for about 25% of the titles published each
year, 30% of the printings and 20% of the volume of publishing
business (6). These figures may be taken as representing a world
average, as France has a highly centralized educational system off-
setting a highly decentralized book industry. In the United States

the concentration of that same industry more than makes up for the educational decentralization which is characteristic of a federal State and the figures are somewhat different, as can be observed in Table II:

TABLE II

The School-book in France and in the United States

	France 1961	United States 1961	1962
Volume of trade			
Total	740,000,000 F	—	$1,608,000,000
School-books	173,000,000 F	—	$409,700,000
Percentage	23·5		25·4
Title production			
Total	11,878	18,060	21,904
School-books	3,025	998	1,421
Percentage	25·5	5·5	6·5
New books			
Total	5,580	14,238	16,448
School-books	650	751	1,032
Percentage	11·6	5·3	6·3
Reprints			
Total	6,298	3,822	5,456
School-books	2,375	247	389
Percentage	37·7	6·5	7·1

The percentage of the volume of trade represented by school-books is almost the same in the United States and in France—*i.e.*, 20 to 25%. Too much importance should not be given to the fact that the American title production of school-books seems to represent a much lower percentage of the total title production than the French. Statistical criteria are entirely different in the two countries, and the American figures refer to hardbound textbooks exclusive of supplementary educational material printed or recorded. It is interesting to note, however, that although school-book publishing in both countries reflects the general trend of the industry, it retains its own specific features. While in the United States new books outnumber reprints by three or four to one and in France reprints are slightly more numerous than new books, percentages show that in both countries school-books give a clear advantage to reprints over new books. This means that the creative element in the school-book is less than in the other types of books.

It is more particularly so in countries endowed with a strongly traditional system of education like Great Britain or France. In such countries, although improvements in the presentation of the school-book may give rise to a sort of communication between its users and producers (7), there are few fields in which stereotypes are so powerful and lasting. Everybody knows the famous book by Sellar and Yeatman, *1066 and All That*, published in 1930, which surveyed with much humour, but also with much truth, the myths which successive editions of history school-books fed five generations of British schoolchildren for over a century. In 1964, another amusing book, by Gaston Bonheur, *Qui a cassé le vase de Soissons?*, did the same for France.

In the United States traditions are less powerful, a fact which accounts for the differences in figures. On the other hand, American school editions are developing at a tremendous rate. As can be seen in Table II, all percentages concerning the school-book have increased by one point in one year, which represents a considerable increase.

Table III shows the increase of the volume of the school-book trade in relation with other factors. The data were drawn from a remarkable article by M. J. Mame, President of the French Centre de Productivité du Livre, published in the *Bibliographie de la France* (No. 21, 25 May 1965, pp. 153 *et seq.*).

TABLE III

School-books in USA : Evolution, 1958–1963

Grade	Number of students	Sales per student	Average price	Volume of trade
Elementary	+14·9%	+ 6·1%	+21·4%	+47·4%
High school	+31·9%	+13·9%	+13·0%	+73·6%
College	+37·8%	+25·0%	+ 5·3%	+84·4%

In fact, the situation is much more fluid in the United States than in any other country. As Edward E. Booher, an American textbook publisher, pointed out in 1961, the textbook—that is, a manual containing texts on which the teacher bases his oral lessons—is disappearing (8). A framework both too rigid and too narrow, it is no longer adaptable to the four major characteristics of modern teaching:

1. The expansion of, and rapid changes in, basic knowledge.

2. The necessary but uncontrollable increase in the number of pupils and students.

3. The need to substitute for the schooling of an élite a system of life-long education permitting all aptitudes to develop fully.

4. The systematic use of audio-visual media as teaching aids.

In short, the same specialization which, during the last few centuries, divorced the functional book from the literary book is now engendering a new, but contrary metamorphosis. As audio-visual media take over the educational role of the scholarly book, the latter is losing much of its functional nature and is ceasing to be merely a teaching machine. Instead of diffusing information according to a preconceived programme within a pre-established network, it can once again *publish* it—that is, make it freely available to an anonymous public.

In 1962, the annual American Publishers' Convention took note of the fact that during the three preceding years an increasing number of schools and universities had adopted paperbacks as books for study (9). This tendency is steadily becoming more pronounced, not only in the United States but throughout the world.

A long time before, Penguin Books had added a functional series, the Pelican Books, to their literary series, and Pelicans have published a large number of high-quality scientific works. It may be added that, for the most part, they have been studies in the sciences of man—archaeology, history, sociology, economics, etc.—probably because these sciences (which were among the last to branch off from literature) are more suitable than others for despecialization. A similar practice has now become common in most of the Western countries, and, in the United States in particular, many scientific texts are published in paperback after having been printed in more expensive bound editions. This, incidentally, is leading university libraries to modify their buying policies accordingly: the working tool thus made available to students and teaching staff ceases to be a fixed and unique reference work, costing all the more because it will soon be outdated, to become part of a constant flow of units of information of all kinds, which are easily replaced and brought up to date as they are used. This continuing give-and-take between scholarly production and consumption already existed in certain series of large-printing semi-popular works which preceded the scientific paperback, such as the famous *Que sais-je?* series in France. Now, especially in the United States, the same publishing technique is currently applied to the major basic textbooks and fundamental scientific works (10).

One result of this change in attitude has been to give the modern paperback edition a certain resemblance to the *incunabula* in the early days of the printed book. It is now possible to find, in the same price range and in similar form, scientific works, joke and crossword-puzzle books, guidebooks, how-to-do-it books, sewing books, cookery books, detective novels, dictionaries, religious books (such as, in France, the *Livre de poche chrétien*), almanacs and reprints of the world's great classics.

The latter are on the border-line between the functional book and the literary book. When, for example, in France, the two publishing houses of Flammarion and Garnier join together to publish the great texts of French and foreign literatures in a paperback series, they are satisfying two different needs: on the one hand, the functional need of schoolchildren and students who find in this series, at the same price but in a much more pleasant form, the set books that they used to obtain in the "classic" editions and, on the other, the literary need of a large number of readers who are discovering a cultural heritage which the high cost and scarcity of the classic editions had previously placed beyond their means.

The literary book

Before proceeding further, we need at least a provisional definition of the literary book. I have been justly criticized because, in my *Sociology of Literature*, published originally in French, in 1958, I gave only a negative definition: "One should understand that literature cannot be defined through any qualitative criterion. My criterion is what I call the search for knowledge for its own sake. Any work which is not functional, but an end in itself is literature. Each act of reading which is not a means to an end, one which satisfies a cultural non-utilitarian need is literature." (11)

Without disavowing that definition, I must concede that it is insufficient. It is one thing to say that the literary book is neither a book-tool nor a book-object, but quite another to say that that is all. As a matter of fact, as I emphasized elsewhere, the literary book can be defined only in terms of a literary *use*: "Real literary motivations respect the 'gratuitousness' of the work and do not use the work as a means but rather as an end. Thus conceived, reading implies solitude even as it excludes solitude. In fact, to read a book as an original creation and not as a tool intended to satisfy a need presupposes *that we go to another person, that we have recourse to someone else,* and thus that we get away from ourselves for a time. In this sense, the companion-book is opposed to the utensil-book, which is completely subordinated to the demands of the individual." (12) I had there the elements of a definition which did not limit the literary book to not serving a practical purpose, but which on the contrary gave it a higher, or at least richer, significance than that of the book-tool. The literary book, I said, presupposes *going to another,* and therefore an exchange. In this exchange lies the criterion which distinguishes the literary from the non-literary. As a matter of fact, I also wrote in the same book, without realizing all that it implied: "We cannot rely on formal classifications or systematic materials to obtain a clear idea of the relation between literature and reading. It is rather the nature of the author-public exchange which may help us to say what litera-ture is—and what it is not. A large number of writings are functional in intention but are generally used in a non-functional and literary way. These occur in newspapers and periodicals as well as in books, often in reporting and in book reviews." (13)   As an example of this, I quoted G. K. Chesterton who, in *The Man Who Was Thursday,* shows that a railway timetable can have a literary use.

In point of fact, there is no such thing as a literary work: there are literary phenomena—that is, dialogues between a writer and various publics. A book may have literary intentions and pretensions—that is, it may call for a dialogue—but it is by no means certain that it will obtain it. On the other hand, a book may have been cast into the void, like the bottle into the sea, and may find the dialogue denied to other books. For this reason, we may say that the charac-teristic of the literary phenomenon is the *existence of a conscious aesthetic judgment* on the part of the reader. In the most favourable circumstances, this judgment is made known to the author either through the critics, through his publisher or, in certain cases, through personal contacts between the author and his public. We know, however, that, since the beginning of the nineteenth century, litera-ture has been marked by a break in contact between the author and the public. From a common-sense point of view, the literary act is the very type of the act of communication: an author transmits to a public, through language, the images and ideas which have arisen in his mind, and in return he receives the praise or the criticism, the indifference or the sympathy of that public. We know already that this pattern, which was valid for the oral teller of tales, no longer applies to the writer and still less to the writer whose works are published and sold in large printings. In our day, communication in literature is primarily a matter of diffusion, one-way diffusion. From the moment his message is sent out—that is to say, from the moment his work is published—the author can no longer change its content, nor control the path it takes, nor decide who is to receive it, nor check that it has been received, nor say how it is to be read and interpreted. It is a journey from which there is no return. On the other hand, when he receives the message thus sent out to him, the anonymous reader can be certain that, unless by an extremely improbable coincidence, the message was not intended specifically and personally for him. He cannot ask for an explanation, an elaboration, a commentary, nor can he imagine the mass of other recipients, and consequently he cannot compare his reactions with theirs (14).

Thus, at both ends of the chain, there is a dual solitude, and it is this solitude which makes the literary act apparently devoid of practical purpose. The absence of a direct, person-to-person link, or at least a mutual awareness of the sending individual and the receiving individual, renders any utilitarian use of the message extremely difficult. It is, of course, not impossible, but it is most problematical and can yield little. The case differs, it should be noted, for the functional book, the school-book for example, whose author and public are very clearly defined in relation one to the other, and whose distribution channels are exactly known. The school-book, as we have seen, has a literary use and significance only when it partakes of the anonymity and unpracticality of the literary book: when an adult browses through a particularly well-illustrated textbook, or when someone interested in old books dwells appreciatively on the artless comments and archaic turns of phrase in a school-book of days gone by.

The solitude of the author and the reader, their mutual unawareness, seem therefore to be inseparable from the literary phenomenon as we know it today. This is the situation which the worn old metaphor of the bottle in the sea seeks to express. The metaphor is, in fact, very imperfect, for it is based on a dangerously romantic interpretation of the shipwrecked sailor's gesture. The sailor makes use of the bottle and the currents of the sea to communicate with rescuers who may come to his aid, because he has no other more perfect, more precise means of communication available to him; but his

SOS is strictly utilitarian and is addressed to a definite person. The most that can be said is that, for the purposes of the image, the gesture may be romanticized and acquire a literary content if, in an adventure story, the message reaches people who can do nothing about it.

Moreover, the bottle has the weakness of being a single thing: the metaphor takes no account of the diffusion, the multiplication of the work which is, whether we will or no, one of the basic features of literature. A better image would be that of the radio signal sent out at random on the air, picked up weakly here and there by a few "hams" and relayed by them all over the planet. It must be admitted that modern techniques have done much to lessen the isolation of those who cry in the wilderness.

They have been without effect upon the solitude of the writer. For him, another metaphor is needed—that, for example, of the trapped pot-holer who pours fluorine into an underground stream, and of the passers-by, the fishermen and watermen, hundreds of miles away, who see the greenish glow of the water and, without suspecting its true origin, wonder uneasily what has caused it. They may admire it or even see it as a supernatural phenomenon.

Must we conclude that no contact is possible between the author and his public? Not at all. There is contact, but the channel by which it is made is not that of the literary work. The dual solitude which we have described above has only a literary existence; it is significant only within the context of literary interchange. The author and the anonymous reader do not exist only as actors therein: both are embedded in a social reality of which they form part, and the contact can be established through that social reality, just as when two conductors of electricity, insulated throughout their length, are short-circuited through the ground.

This brings us back to the underlying significance of such ideas as "humanism" and "commitment". These are often interpreted as moral values destined to replace aesthetic values or, at least, to unite with them in the creation of a work. The result is an irreconcilable conflict between the demands of the "message" and the demands of art. In point of fact, to say that a writer is a "humanist" does not mean that he gives any special philosophical touch to his work or that he puts into it the wisdom drawn from much reading; and to say that a writer is "committed" does not mean that he uses his work for ideological purposes, that he intends it, feels and thinks of it as an instrument, a means of action. Both terms merely seek to express the fact that the writer in question is deeply rooted in a collective reality, whatever that reality may be. They seek to express the idea that in him the social man is completely identified with the poetic creator. In defining literature, Jean-Paul Sartre was right in asking for whom the writer writes (15). The exteriorization which is the essence of the composition of a literary work is meaningful only if it is done for or before someone. Even if we personify an inanimate object (such as Midas's barber's hole in the ground or the microphone of a tape-recorder), or speak to an animal, some hypothetical listener is necessary. The listener acts as a sound-box; his function is twofold, for he plays a part, firstly, as the determinant in the creation of the work which is formulated with him in mind, and secondly, as the intermediary between the work and the anonymous public, since it is his presence and the writer's imagination which give a literary significance to the confidence or the confession. On him, then, depends the social richness of the work—that is, the number, intensity and quality of the "earth" connections between the author and his readers.

It is obvious that the more intense the author's "humanism" or "committedness" or any other quality implying a multiplicity of social ties, the more "vibrant" will be the listener to whom he addresses himself and whose language he speaks. He will therefore be more likely to speak the language, fulfil the expectations, and satisfy the need of an ordinary reader. Moreover, this ordinary reader, to the extent that he partakes of the social nature of the hypothetical listener (and the richer that nature is, the more likely will he be to partake of it), also plays a part in determining the work: we may say that he makes himself heard by the author in advance.

Therefore, even if there is no visible contact between the author and his public, exchange and communication nevertheless take place between them, provided that the hypothetical public for which the work is intended represents a sufficient richness of social life on the part of the author.

But this is not all. The organization of literary life, as it tends to be established in highly-developed societies, promotes or hampers communication between the writer and the public. The literary phenomenon, to be complete, requires not only that the writer deliver to the reader a message which is intelligible, or at least usable, but also that the reasoned judgment of the reader be, in one way or another, reflected back to the writer, either directly or through the publisher who indirectly governs what he produces. In other words, the key to the literary phenomenon lies in whether or not there is a literary public opinion—that is, in the public's awareness of its tastes, preferences, needs and attitudes. It lies in the expression of that opinion, in the way it is transmitted at the level of the literary producers and entrepreneurs—that is to say, the writers and publishers. Its expression must be clear enough to be understood, but discreet enough not to be coercive and not to inhibit the necessary freedom of literary creation.

The entire critical apparatus, the entire "literary life" of most countries in our day, tends to restrict literary public opinion to that of a single social level, and usually of a single class. This is nothing new. As we have seen, indeed, the history of the book is the history of the participation of ever more numerous strata of the population in the literary exchange. There has always been a "lettered" literature, involving conscious exchanges between certain publics and certain writers, alongside a literature "bestowed" or "imposed", which is merely the anonymous consumption of reading matter by masses whose numbers and composition have varied from one century to another.

We are only just beginning to suspect the importance of this "sub-literature" existing alongside "good literature". Yet there are many ties between them. Certain literary forms which originated in one have been transferred to the other as societies have evolved and, most important, as the organization of the cultural life of these societies has permitted this to happen. Thus, comedies, novels and songs were all, at certain times in their history, regarded as being sub-literary, and were promoted to a higher status only with the promotion of their readers. More recently, the detective novel has undergone a similar mutation. It is not unreasonable to suppose that, one day, even the despised and disparaged strip-cartoon will be accepted as a literary *genre* when its habitual readers have acquired the intellectual and material means, first to formulate an aesthetic judgment on the comic strip and thereafter to make that judgment heard and to take part in the operation of the literary process (16).

Alongside literature, therefore, we must also consider the immense field of what is sometimes called sub-literature, or infra-literature or marginal literature. On the edge of this field is the place of the literary book visibly determined not only by aesthetic, but also

—and mainly—by social factors. It is understandable, for instance, that a book's "literariness" may depend on the public for which it is intended, and the recent phenomenon of the paperback brings sharply to our attention the problem of the semi-literary on the fringe of the literary. Now, suddenly, books which had been born within a certain social group, which had been judged and approved, have been brought to new and unsuspected readers as a result of large printings. Until this happened, the literature "bestowed" was a sub-literature, a secondary or industrial product, as it were, intended for consumption by anonymous masses. But, suddenly, the literature which a certain social group had recognized as being "good" has been made available to other social groups which did not call it into being and which have no means of making known their opinion of it. Steinbeck is sold in drugstores, and Camus in "chain-stores", but the customers of the drugstore and the "chain-store" have no way of participating in the exchange which can give rise to new Steinbecks and a new Camus. So far as the future of written culture is concerned, this is probably the most disquieting and the most difficult problem created by the modern publishing revolution.

NOTES

(1) A survey carried out from January to April, 1960, under the sponsorship of the National Association of French Publishers showed that 9% of the persons interviewed had read 11 or more books between 1 December 1959 and 1 March 1960. A similar survey conducted in Derby in 1953 by T. Cauter and J. S. Downham (*The Communication of Ideas*, London, 1954, pp. 190–3) showed that 10% of the persons interviewed had read more than 4 books during the preceding month. Since in both cases no previous definition of a 'book' was agreed upon, the figures cannot be relied on too heavily. Yet they allow us to consider a book a week as an 'average' consumption, for the group concerned.

(2) In a survey conducted at the Army Induction Centre at Limoges in December 1962 and January 1963, by the Centre de Sociologie des Faits littéraires de Bordeaux, it was found that 20% of the young recruits stated that they had more than 50 books in their homes. J. Dumazedier's well-known Annecy survey showed that 20% of Annecy homes had libraries of over 150 books. In Derby, T. Cauter and J. S. Downham (*op. cit.*, pp. 194–5) found that 20% of the

persons interviewed had 100 or more books in their homes, while a similar study made in the United States in 1947 found that 29% of the persons interviewed gave the same answer. On the other hand, Peter Meyer-Dohm, in *Der Westdeutsche Büchermarkt* (Stuttgart, 1957, p. 123), quotes a 1955 survey conducted in the Federal Republic of Germany and West Berlin by the Allesbascher Institüt für Demoskopie, according to which only 10% of the persons interviewed had 100 or more books in their homes. These differences, however, are not significant since the wording of the question was in each case different and no previous definition of a 'book' was given. Roughly speaking, we may suggest that people reading a book a week and owning 100 books or more represent about the same proportion of the reading public.

(3) See my article, R. Escarpit, *Le problème de l'âge dans la productivité littéraire*, in *Bulletin des bibliothèques de France*, 5e année, No. 5, May 1960, pp. 105–11, and the paper I presented at the Symposium on the Sociology of Literature, Brussels, 22 May 1964, on *L'image historique de la littérature chez les jeunes*.

(4) Data provided by J. Dumazedier and J. Hassenforder, *Eléments pour une sociologie comparée de la production, de la diffusion et de l'utilisation du livre*, Paris, 1962, p. 40. See also *Etudes sur la distribution du livre en France* by the Centre d'Etudes du Commerce, Paris, 1960.

(5) P. Riberette, *Les clubs du livre*, *Bulletin des bibliothèques de France*, 1ère année, No. 6, June 1956, p. 425.

(6) *Techniques graphiques* (Paris), No. 34, December 1960, *Le livre scolaire en France*, p. 31, and *Monographie de l'Edition*, Paris, Cercle de la Librairie, 1963, pp. 58 *et seq.*

(7) R. Escarpit, *Sociologie du livre scolaire*, in *Techniques graphiques*, (Paris), No. 34, December 1960, pp. 74–75.

(8) Edward E. Booher, *Books and Their Market Twenty-five Years from Now*, in *Publishers' Weekly* (Philadelphia), vol. 179, No. 10, 6 March 1961, pp. 20 *et seq.*

(9) *Current Comments on Paperbacks*, in *Library Journal* (Philadelphia), vol. 87, No. 16, 15 September 1963, p. 2981.

(10) See Frank L. Schick, *The Paperbound Book in America*, New York, 1958, *passim*. Chapter 13 includes a study of paperbacks published by universities. Certain series are very well known: Great Seal Books (Cornell University Press), Midland Books (Indiana Uni-

versity Press), Phoenix Books (University of Chicago Press), Ann
Arbor Paperbacks (University of Michigan Press), etc.

(11) R. Escarpit, *Sociology of Literature*, Painesville, Ohio, 1965, p. 14.

(12) *Ibid.*, pp. 90–91.

(13) *Ibid.*, p. 15.

(14) This topic is discussed in greater detail in my article, *L'acte littéraire est-il un acte de communication?* in *Filoloski Pregled*, Belgrade, 1963, 1–2, pp. 17–21.

(15) J.-P. Sartre, *Qu'est-ce que la littérature?*, Paris, 1947.

(16) This problem is referred to in my paper, *Y a-t-il des degrés dans la littérature?* in *Actes du Ve Congrès national de littérature comparée*, Paris, 1965.

PART TWO

The New Look in Publishing

World Production

Interpretation of statistical data

THE difficulty of classifying books and the impossibility of defining them precisely makes the task of preparing and interpreting publishing statistics an extremely hazardous one. Back in 1956, R. E. Barker drew attention to the very wide range of criteria adopted in various countries for defining a book (1). In Italy, for example, a volume must consist of at least 100 pages if it is to be regarded as a book, whereas no such stipulation exists in India. Most countries based their definition of a book on the number of pages, while the United Kingdom's criterion was a minimum price.

Fortunately, agreement has recently been reached on an international definition of a book. A "Recommendation concerning the international standardization of statistics relating to book production and periodicals" was adopted by the General Conference of Unesco on 19 November 1964. Prepared over a long period, this Recommendation should—if it is observed by all States—solve the problem for the future by the adoption of uniform definitions. A *book* is "a non-periodical printed publication of at least 49 pages, exclusive of the cover pages". A *pamphlet* is "a non-periodical printed publication of at least 5 but not more than 48 pages, exclusive of the cover pages". The Recommendation also defines a *first edition*, a *re-edition*, a *reprint*, a *translation*, and a *title*, and contains detailed suggestions regarding classification, methods of enumeration and the different sorts of statistics that should be drawn up annually at the national level. It provides that the following categories should be excluded from the statistics: 1, publications issued for advertising purposes, 2, publications of a transitory character, and 3, publications in which the text is not the most important part.

It is, therefore, very much to be hoped that in the fairly near future this Recommendation will eliminate the shortcomings of the statistics at present available. For the time being, we can only feel our way and try to discover trends and tendencies. The main thing is that we should have a clear idea of what we can learn from the various data now at our disposal (2).

The most easily established and commonest statistics concern titles published. Most countries have a system of "duty copies" whereby all publishers are obliged to provide the authorities with one or more copies of each book produced.

It is therefore simple to obtain some idea of publishers' activities by referring to the list of books which they have deposited during the year. It should, however, be noted that statistics of this kind based on titles merely give us the number of publishing ventures without supplying any information on the economic magnitude of such ventures or, above all, on their cultural content. Not every publishing venture implies a "venture" by a writer, a new intellectual or artistic achievement. This "real" production can be arrived at only by deducting re-issues and translations from the gross figure. A certain number of countries do one or the other in their statistics but rarely both, and this, needless to say, makes comparisons no easier. Until the Unesco Recommendation is generally adopted, we remain ill-informed about the number of "first editions". It is beginning to be possible to evaluate the number of translations, thanks to the details given in the *Index Translationum* published by Unesco. Only by combining the two sets of figures could we obtain a relatively close interpretation of the overall statistics based on titles. And even then, for this operation to be really valid, we should have to be able to carry it out in respect of each class of publication, and more especially, in respect of Class 8, comprising books classified as literature. As things stand, however, this is an unattainable dream. At best we can make a few evaluations which are as conjectural as they are unreliable.

From the economic standpoint, evaluations are even less reliable, since words have different meanings in the socialist countries and in the capitalist countries. The latter accord an overriding importance to business and include only commercial publications in their figures. The United States, for example, does not include Government publications which are distributed free, this criterion, incidentally, being unsatisfactory, since volumes purchased by the State from private publishers and distributed free for purposes of aid or propaganda are included in the statistics. Should the same discrimination be made in respect of production in the USSR where commercial channels do not have the same meaning as in the United States? Soviet production may vary by more than 20%, depending on whether or not this is done.

The most exact means of evaluation would be to combine statistics based on titles and statistics based on editions—*i.e.*, on the number of copies printed. These are comparable physical data providing information both about the economic importance of publishing activity and the place which this holds in the life of the country.

Unfortunately, the position as regards editions is scarcely any better than in respect of titles. It is true that some progress has been made since the days when publishers regarded such information as a trade secret. Nowadays it is possible to gain at least an approximate idea of the number of copies printed in the main producer countries. The socialist countries have never made any great secret of this. Elsewhere, the veil is beginning to be lifted, and it is now possible to make evaluations which are something more than mere hypotheses. To guide us in making such evaluations, to confirm them and even, in certain cases, to go further, we can refer to the data published by the international organizations concerning the consumption of printing- and writing-paper. There is, of course, no fixed relation between book production and the consumption of such paper, but, as in the case of statistics based on titles, comparison of the figures from year to year gives some idea of the main trends, which can be compared with those detected or identified in other fields.

The picture thus obtained of the publishing situation would be incomplete if left in the form of a juxtaposition of national statistics. Here, a third series of data must be taken into account—*i.e.*, those concerning the "dynamics" of publishing, in other words figures relating to translations, exports and imports, joint editions and, generally speaking, cultural exchanges. As we have already seen, books represent the most convenient and effective method for the dissemination of thought and art. They are above all characterized by mobility, movement and circulation. Static information concerning titles and editions must therefore be combined with dynamic information on the great movements which are now transforming the book market from a national into a world-wide affair.

Gross statistics by titles

The following table shows global production by titles in the various countries for 1962 or for the year closest to 1962 for which such information has been published. In these cases, the reference year is shown in brackets.

In order to facilitate comparison and to bring out some of the main trends in world publishing, figures are also given for 1952 or the nearest possible year. This ten-year interval is sufficient for the purposes of a comparative study.

TABLE IV

World Production by Titles
Evolution from 1952 to 1962

COUNTRY	1952	1962
Afghanistan	—	60 (63)
Albania	98	571
Argentina	4,257	3,323
Australia	627	1,793
Austria	3,179	3,557
Belgium	4,610	3,465
Brazil	3,208	3,911 (61)
Bulgaria	2,031	3,716 (61) or 3,767 (63)
Burma	82 (51)	330 (60)
Cambodia	392 (53)	159
Cameroons	—	18
Canada	684	3,600
Ceylon	268	1,969
Chile	—	1,040
China (Taiwan)	427	2,625
China (Mainland)	2,507	26,414 (58)
Costa Rica	—	164
Cuba	615 (53)	736
Czechoslovakia	5,837	8,703
Denmark	2,186	4,157
Dominican Republic	115 (49)	71 (63)
El Salvador	—	139
Ethiopia	—	178 (61)
Finland	1,748	2,646

COUNTRY	*1952*	*1962*
France*	11,954	13,282
Germany (Federal Republic)	13,913	21,481
Germany (Eastern)	4,310 (53)	6,540
Ghana	—	269 (63)
Greece	1,016	1,277
Guatemala	70 (53)	500
Guinea	—	4 (63)
Honduras	70 (53)	189
Hungary	3,195	5,256
Iceland	420	665 (59)
India	18,252	11,086
Indonesia	778	869 (61)
Iran	391 (54)	569 (61)
Iraq	248 (53)	143 (59)
Ireland	149	217
Israel	822 (50)	2,532 (61)
Italy	8,949	7,401 (61)
Japan	17,306	22,010
Jordan	—	162 (63)
Kenya	—	98
Korea (Republic of)	1,393	3,720
Kuwait	—	161 (63)
Lebanon	396 (50)	402
Liberia	—	4 (60)
Libya	—	5 (60)
Luxembourg	420	134 (61)
Malaysia	—	338
Mexico	—	3,760
Monaco	104	38
Morocco	100	161 (60)
Netherlands	6,728	9,674
New Zealand	327	1,212
Nicaragua	122 (47)	—
Nigeria	—	262 (63)
Norway	2,704	3,119
Pakistan	—	1,787
Panama	22	—
Peru	702	791

* The figures for 1952 and 1962 include the total production of books (locally produced works, translations, publications in foreign languages) represented by the 'duty copies' deposited and listed in the *Bibliographie de la France* and the *Annuaire Statistique de la France*. (Source: Unesco.)

COUNTRY	*1952*	*1962*
Philippines	195 (53)	595 (63)
Poland	6,632	7,162
Portugal	4,153	4,461
Rhodesia	—	369
Rumania	5,381 (53)	7,359
Rwanda	—	23
Saudi Arabia	—	321
Senegal	—	67
Sierra Leone	—	48
Singapore	—	237
South Africa	834	1,289 (63)
Spain	3,445	9,556
Sudan	—	83 (63)
Sweden	3,286	5,472
Switzerland	3,245	5,633
Thailand	3,953	1,397 (61)
Tunisia	56 (53)	—
Turkey	2,447	4,842
Uganda	—	46 (63)
Union of Soviet Socialist Republics	43,135	79,140
United Arab Republic	654 (53)	3,294
United Kingdom of Great Britain	18,741	25,079
United States	11,840	21,904
Uruguay	—	217
Venezuela	—	338 (61) or 743 (63)
Viet-Nam (Republic of)	936	1,515
Yugoslavia	5,184	5,637
Zanzibar	—	75

The first point emerging from this table is that there are certain publishing "giants". Six countries produce more than 20,000 titles a year: the USSR, mainland China, the United Kingdom, Germany (whether we take the Federal Republic separately or in conjunction with Eastern Germany), Japan and the United States. Six other countries come near to 10,000 titles: France, India, Spain, Italy, the Netherlands and Czechoslovakia. These twelve countries alone account for three-quarters of the world production, which Unesco estimated at 400,000 titles in 1963.

Obviously certain adjustments must be made to this list. The almost 80,000 books published in the USSR are not all books in the

Western sense of the word. Moreover, many Soviet titles are counted several times, since the figure does not relate solely to Russian-language books but to cumulated production in ninety-three languages, sixty-one of them being the languages of peoples within the Soviet Union and thirty-two foreign languages (3). The fact remains, however, that even if only works published in Russian and intended for distribution through normal commercial channels were to be counted, Soviet production would still exceed 30,000 titles, making it the highest in the world.

We have already indicated how it happens that India is among the main producers: the Indian definition of a book means that even the smallest pamphlet can be considered as belonging to that category. In actual fact, India should be placed in a very much lower bracket.

So far as Spain is concerned, it first won a leading place in 1962, with an output of 9,556 titles. Figures for earlier years, although showing a steady increase, were lower: 5,761 in 1959, 6,085 in 1960, 6,819 in 1961. A sudden rise of 40% seems, at first sight, abnormal. It is difficult to say whether it is a question of a transitory phenomenon or a basic trend.

Italy once more suffers from its own unduly rigorous definition of books and should in fact be placed on an equal footing with France, and the same probably applies to Czechoslovakia. As far as mainland China is concerned, we have no precise information about the criteria used for classification.

If we compare the figures for 1952 and 1962, it is apparent that, while world production as a whole increased by some 40%, production in several countries declined over the same period. Except for India (and, once again, figures on Indian production are perhaps not entirely comparable because of divergent definitions), none of these countries is among the big producers. Among medium-sized producers, however, mention may be made of Belgium, where production dropped by 25%, and Italy, where there was a decline of 16%. Countries which remained stable—*i.e.*, where production either did not vary or increased in roughly the same proportion as world production—include France with 5·3%, Austria with 11%, Japan with 27% and the United Kingdom with 35%. But it is where the increase in production exceeds 40% that we find the most spectacular advances. In mainland China, for example, production increased more than tenfold in six years. The United States, with an increase of 85%, is now directly rivalling Japan for fourth place, whereas, ten years earlier, it came sixth, or approximately at the same level as France. This new importance acquired by English-speaking America, which will be discussed later, is confirmed by the increase of Canadian production which, in ten years, rose from 684 to 3,600 titles—*i.e.*, an increase of 426·2%. A general regrouping is visibly taking place, even though the former centre of balance has not yet been displaced.

Examination of the above table likewise reveals the existence of blocs or groups which should be considered as a whole. The most immediately apparent are the language groups. So far as a common language creates intellectual exchanges, it may be considered that the publishing industries in those countries which use the same language as a literary or, at any rate, intellectual medium of expression, are interdependent. We shall have to come back to this idea of language groups when we discuss reading, at which point we shall need to evaluate the absorptive capacity of each of those groups. At this stage, we are concerned only with establishing the respective importance of the various languages in world production.

There are twelve literary languages commonly used by more than 50,000,000 people. In order of importance these are Chinese, English, Russian, Hindi, Spanish, German, Japanese, Bengali, Arabic, French, Portuguese and Italian. Japanese, Italian and Portuguese may be left aside for the moment since they are used for literary production which is strictly limited to certain territories (the Japanese Archipelago, the Italian peninsula, Portugal and Brazil). We shall also set aside the case of Chinese, since information on this is still very sparse and since, notwithstanding its physical and human range, it is, so to speak, *sui generis*. As regards the Indian languages and Arabic, although the countries concerned are steadily advancing in the cultural field, their publishing industries are still too small and too dispersed for us to be able to speak of genuine groups. Finally, so far as there is a "Soviet" nationality, Russian is an infra-national rather than a supra-national language. This case will be discussed at a later stage.

We are therefore left with the four great Western supra-national languages: English, German, Spanish and French. Around these, linguistic groups have come into being which vary in size and nature. The English group comprises two great economic powers, the United States and the United Kingdom, and takes in all the countries belonging to the British Commonwealth. The Spanish group resembles the English in that it is widely spread (since it involves two continents), but the component nations are economically weaker and culturally less developed than those of the English group. The French group likewise has overseas ramifications (Canada, Haiti, West Indies and Africa), but its real strength comes from Europe and mainly from France. Of the other French-speaking countries, Belgium contributes roughly two-fifths of its book production and Switzerland between one-sixth and one-fifth. Lastly, the German group, which is the most homogeneous, covers only Central Europe, where it is based on the two Germanys, Austria, German-speaking Switzerland and a certain number of German-speaking minorities in various other countries. The following table shows (in round figures) the gross production, by titles, for the four groups in 1952 and 1962. A separate column for each of the two years shows the percentage in relation to world production.

TABLE V

The Language Groups

	1952	%	1962	%
World production	250,000	100	350,000*	100
English group	32,000	12·8	55,000	15·7
German group	25,000	10·0	35,000	10·0
Spanish group	14,000	5·6	20,000	5·7
French group	14,000	5·6	15,000	4·3
Total	85,000	34·0	125,000	35·7

* The figure of 350,000 for 1962, like that of the 370,000 estimated for 1964, is based only on data verified and reproduced in the tables of this volume. The Unesco estimates for the total number of titles produced throughout the world are: 360,000 for 1960, 375,000 for 1961, 385,000 for 1962 and 400,000 for 1963.

It will be noted that the total production of the four groups occupies approximately the same place in world production in 1952 and in 1962. It seems to show a slight rising trend, but this cannot be considered significant in view of the narrow change involved and the fact that the figures used are not absolutely exact. Broadly speaking, if we take world production in 1952 as amounting to 250,000 titles, and in 1962 to 350,000 titles, then the four groups together accounted for 34% of this production in 1952 and approximately 36% in 1962.

But while the overall situation may not have changed greatly, the same cannot be said of the balance among the groups. Although the production of no individual group has declined in absolute terms, the gaps between the groups have widened noticeably. The English group accounted for some 13% of production in 1952 and about 16% in 1962, which is quite a marked increase, since the group thus registered an advance of nearly 70%, representing a rate of growth double that of the world rate. Conversely, at the other extreme, the French group, with a rate of growth of about 7%, declined relatively, even if only to a slight extent. The German and Spanish groups, for their part, maintained their positions.

These shifts within the scale, however, mean nothing unless we look at what is actually taking place within the groups. Table IV tends to indicate a sort of concentration within the French-, German-, and Spanish-language groups on what might be called the "focal language" countries. Thus production is rising faster in Germany than in Austria; in France than in Belgium or Monaco; in Spain than in Spanish-speaking America. This magnetic attraction phenomenon will cause no surprise to literary historians. It has been noted that literary life in our day is tending to undergo regrouping across national frontiers. Although a Belgian literature is not thereby ceasing to exist, it is certain that Belgian authors writing in French are thinking of themselves more and more as belonging to French literature or, at any rate, as taking part in French literary life. A similar movement towards the Netherlands may be seen in the small Dutch-Flemish linguistic group.

An entirely different process is taking place within the English group. Here, there are two centres—the United Kingdom and the United States—and a phenomenon is now occurring of which English publishers have stood in fear ever since the heroic period when Dickens went to the United States to defend the rights of British authors. The United States is gradually taking the United Kingdom's place at the head of the language group. In 1952 the United Kingdom, with some 18,700 titles, still accounted for considerably more than half of the group's total production. In 1962, with some 25,000 titles, it accounted for a little less than half, and the United States came close behind with approximately 22,000 titles. Lastly, and perhaps even more important, the Commonwealth was insignificant in 1952 as far as publishing was concerned, whereas ten years later it produced more than 6,500 titles, a far from negligible figure, so that it is now beginning to weigh heavily in the balance. It may be worth pointing out that the sharp rise in United States production is largely due to the mass publication of paperbacks.

Let us look now at the other main group, with the Russian language as its nucleus. Here it is no longer a question of a linguistic group, but of the group made up of socialist countries among which there are frequent and systematic exchanges so that their publishing activities are, to a certain extent, interdependent. It is interesting that in 1962 the production of these countries—not including mainland China—almost exactly equalled that of the four Western language groups discussed above. It amounted to approximately 125,000 titles—i.e., 36% of world production. But the rise in production within the socialist countries had been quicker, since ten years earlier it amounted to only 75,000 titles—i.e., 30%. The advance is sufficiently marked to merit recording.

It demonstrates, in any case, that the share left to the developing countries decreased considerably over ten years—from 36% to 28%. This trend, however, will probably change in the years ahead. Once again, Table IV shows that nearly twenty new nations entered the lists over the ten years and it may be assumed that their numbers will increase and that their output will also rise. Of the forty nations mentioned in Table IV which do not belong to any of the groups so far considered, thirty-one are Afro-Asian nations, most of them having only recently emerged, and nine are European nations with an ancient culture and a publishing industry firmly rooted in tradition. The rate of growth in the production of the nine European nations between 1952 and 1962, however, was barely 25%, and hence lower than the world rate, whereas in the case of the thirty-one Afro-Asian nations it was 33%. No definite conclusions can as yet be drawn from these figures, but it is very probable that the phase of concentration into linguistic and ideological blocs will shortly be followed by a phase of expansion outwards to the young nations, which will profoundly change the face of publishing throughout the world.

Statistics by number of copies

In 1954, R. E. Barker estimated the number of books printed annually throughout the world at five thousand million. This figure seems somewhat too high. We estimate the number of titles published in 1952 at 250,000. The figure for 1954 should be in the region of 270,000. Barker's estimate could be accepted only if we assumed that the average number of copies of each title published was 20,000. It is true that editions exceeding 20,000 are not unusual, but there are very few countries where this figure could be regarded as an average, and, in any case, it could not be taken as a world average.

The USSR, for example, with a population of over 220,000,000 and an illiteracy rate of only 2%, with an economic structure which enables its publishing industry to ignore considerations of commercial profit, officially recorded 1,248,800,000 copies for 79,140 titles published in 1962. This represents an average edition of 15,748 copies per title. The highest average number of copies ever reported by the USSR was that of 1954: 997,000,000 copies for 50,100 titles —*i.e.*, 19,900 copies per title. In the interests of strict accuracy, however, it should be noted that if the figures for the Russian Soviet Federal Socialist Republic are taken alone, the average number of copies printed is slightly more than 20,000.

The French Publishers Association gave the figure of 178,667,000 copies, representing 11,878 titles, for 1959 (4)—*i.e.*, an average per title of 15,041, which is of the same order as that of the USSR.

Moreover, in drawing up the table of book production by number of copies in each country, R. E. Barker himself used figures comparable with those given above (5). His estimates for the main producer countries for 1952 were as follows:

USSR	17,300 copies per title
United Kingdom	15,200 copies per title
United States	13,900 copies per title
France	9,700 copies per title
Federal Republic of Germany	7,700 copies per title

The other countries he lists are shown as having editions of between 3,000 and 6,000 copies per title.

It may reasonably be assumed, therefore, that the average printing per title on a world basis is in the region of 10,000 copies, which would reduce the number of copies printed throughout the world in 1952 to 2,500 million. The world average has undoubtedly risen since then: not only is the greater number of writers and the increased importance of the publishing industry reflected in a larger number of titles, but, by the same token, the rise in readership due to population growth and the decline in illiteracy has led to bigger printings. It would seem, moreover, that the increase in both sectors is about equal—*i.e.*, some 30%. If we consider the rise in the consumption of printing- and writing-paper throughout the world over the ten years, it may be supposed that the average printing in 1962 was in fact about 13,000 copies, which would give a total production for 1962 of 4,500 million copies—not much less than the 5,000 million copies announced somewhat prematurely by R. E. Barker.

The data provided by the figures on printing- and writing-paper consumption enable us to make certain somewhat daring extrapolations.

We shall take it, as a hypothesis, that the paper consumption in a given country depends both upon the number of works published and upon the average printing of each of those works, and that variations in consumption are related in part to the variations of these two factors. In a few cases we can find out the variations in production by titles. If these are of the same order as the variations in paper consumption and show a similar trend, it may be concluded that the average edition is remaining stationary. If consumption of paper is seen to be increasing more rapidly than production by numbers of titles, it may be assumed that the size of the editions is increasing. Conversely, if consumption is increasing less rapidly, it may be assumed that the size of editions is declining. Table VI (overleaf) shows printing- and writing-paper consumption in various countries in 1955 side by side with production by titles in the same countries for the same year. In order to highlight the variation, the figures have been related to a common basis of 100, representing the last pre-war year for which data are available.

It should be borne in mind that what we are after here is not an exact evaluation but merely an indication of a general trend. In most countries the difference between the variations is striking and reflects a very distinct increase in the size of average editions, bearing out what we have already learnt. On the other hand, the United Kingdom remains completely stable: the number of titles produced increases on the same scale as paper consumption.

It must be pointed out forthwith that the trends may well have changed since 1955. It is only since then that the impact of paperbacks has made itself really felt in respect of American editions,

whereas this type of publication already existed in Great Britain
before the War.

It is difficult to carry the interpretation of these data any further,
and it goes without saying that no constant relation applying to all
countries can be found between book production and the consumption of printing- and writing-paper for the excellent reason that such
paper, always reckoned separately from newsprint, is not used solely

TABLE VI

Variations in Paper Consumption and Book Production
1955 in relation to 1938
(1938=100)

Country	Consumption of printing-paper (other than newsprint) and writing-paper	Book Production (by titles)
Netherlands	240	119
United States	189	113
France	179	128
Italy	151	101
Switzerland	362	177
Japan	122	70
United Kingdom	118	123
Spain	105	389

(Source: Unesco.)

for the manufacture of books. Besides consumption in the form of
exercise-books and writing-paper, it is also used for the production
of periodicals and magazines. The proportion used for books therefore depends on the place held by periodicals in the country concerned. Table VII provides a striking illustration of this fact. The
figures for numbers of copies printed, as calculated by Barker for
1952, have simply been multiplied by 0·4 to obtain the weight (W)
of paper consumed in book production within each country, the
average weight of a book being in fact about 400 grammes. Additionally, the total consumption (C) of printing- and writing-paper in
the same countries has been estimated, and, finally, C has been
divided by W to determine whether there is a constant coefficient by
which W can be derived from C.

In the case of the European countries with a cultural life of the
same kind—*i.e.*, Belgium, France, the Federal Republic of Germany

and the United Kingdom—there is definitely a common coefficient which would seem to be in the region of 7 or 8. As far as the United States is concerned, however, the coefficient is entirely different, amounting to 66—*i.e.*, almost ten times that of the European countries. There is nothing surprising in this. Commenting on figures obtained elsewhere and by other methods, in my *Sociology of Literature* I pointed out that the readership of magazines in the United States was ten times greater than in Europe, where the coefficient was in fact the one established here: "In France in 1955,

TABLE VII

Relation between Paper Consumption and Number of Copies published

Country	Number of copies published (in millions)	Weight of copies (W) in thousands of tons	Total consumption (C) in thousands of tons	$\dfrac{C}{W}$
France	100	40	340	8·5
Federal Republic of Germany	108	43	340	7·9
United Kingdom	286	114	750	6·6
Belgium	26	10	80	8·0
United States	165	66	4,400	66·0

out of 10·6 kilograms of paper for writing and printing consumed *per capita*, the book industry's consumption was roughly 1·4 kilograms." (6)

Has this situation changed to any great extent since 1951 or 1952? As far as France is concerned, certainly not. According to figures provided by the French Publishers Association (7), French publishers' consumption of paper in 1958 amounted to approximately 1·1 kilo per head of population and in 1962 to 1·3, corresponding to the increase in the overall consumption of printing- and writing-paper.

The situation in the United States is quite different. In ten years, the consumption of paper has increased by 50%, but the proportion going to books has increased to a much greater extent. After more than a century of dominance, magazines have had to make way for books, and such major companies as *Life* and *Reader's Digest* have launched out on book production by the large-scale methods to which they already owed their success. Since 1955, big business has broken into American publishing and has transformed the scale of the industry. A modern paperback publisher takes the view that an edition of less than 100,000 is not worth while. In 1960 it was estimated that 1,000,000 paperbacks were sold each day in the United States. The figures given in 1957 by Chandler B. Grannis (8) are significant, especially if we bear in mind the 164,000,000 copies of 1952:

Ordinary books for adults	115,000,000 copies
Children's books	120,000,000 copies
School-books	130,000,000 copies
Paperbacks	200,000,000 copies

Such is the extent of the paperback revolution in the United States. These mass-production methods would seem destined to spread to other countries, including the European countries. Is it, then, to be feared that in this field, too, American industrial power is imposing its methods on the rest of the world and, in the case of book publishing, combining economic conquest with cultural conquest and thus helping to stifle the voice of countries which are not yet fully developed? As we have already seen, the share of such countries in production by titles has declined relatively in recent years. If we examine the consumption of printing- and writing-paper in those parts of the world where publishing is still too little developed for the printing figures to be genuinely significant, we shall perhaps be able to make a cautious guess at some of the future trends of publishing there.

Table VIII, opposite, recapitulates printing- and writing-paper consumption in the various regions of the world between 1950 and 1960. The trends seem to be clear and confirm our previous observations. The most striking feature is the decline of English-speaking America which in 1950 accounted for more than half of world consumption but, in 1960, for only 43·2%. Europe and Latin America remained at the same level, whereas Oceania—basically Australia and New Zealand—showed a slight advance. The most spectacular progress, however, was that of the Afro-Asian countries—an increase of 242·5% for Africa and 512·3% for Asia. It should be noted, moreover, that this advance was not restricted to such economically strong countries as Japan and China, but also extended over the whole of this vast region where, in ten years, the *per capita* consumption of printing- and writing-paper in such countries as Burma, Cambodia, Iraq and Israel increased tenfold, the extreme case being probably that of Syria, where *per capita* consumption rose from

0·01 kilo per year in 1950 to 0·3 in 1960—an increase of 3,000%! The same applies to Africa, where consumption in a country with a large European population—South Africa—rose from 34,000 tons to only 47,000 tons in ten years, while for the rest of Africa—*i.e.*, the recently independent countries—it rose from 6,000 tons in 1950 to 90,000 in 1960.

TABLE VIII

Consumption of Printing- and Writing-paper in Various Regions of the World

Evolution between 1950 and 1960

Region	1950 Consumption in 1,000 of tons	1950 Percentage of world consumption	1960 Consumption in 1,000 of tons	1960 Percentage of world consumption	Variation in consumption
Europe	2,591	34·5	5,145	36·1	+ 98·6%
English-speaking America	4,245	56·5	6,150	43·2	+ 44·9%
Latin America	220	2·9	435	3·0	+ 97·7%
Africa	40	0·5	137	1·0	+242·5%
Asia	365	4·8	2,235	15·7	+512·3%
Oceania	60	0·8	141	1·0	+135·0%
Total	7,521	100	14,243	100	+89·4%

(Source: *The Place of Paper in Development and Foreign Aid*, International Institute for Economic Studies, University of Stockholm, 1963.)

These 90,000 tons do not represent much in the world economy, just as African literature does not yet count for much in world culture, but they show that African books, which prior to decolonization represented 1 in 20 in their own region, rose in ten years to the point where the ratio became 2 to 1 in their favour.

Literary books

All the foregoing observations apply to books in general, in other words to books considered as manufactured products, consumer goods, trade items, without reference either to their content or to the use made of them. Obviously, however, the problems differ greatly as between functional books and literary books. The very nature of the functional book means that its evolution and development are linked with economic, technical and scientific activities concerning which we are generally fairly well informed. School-books, for example, reflect the trends in the educational system for which they are designed, technical books reflect the concern of a developing or expanding economy, social science books directly express the directions taken by a given political system.

Literary books are linked with literature as such, in other words with the most elusive and indefinable of all realities. None the less, it is this reality which we must try to pin down, it is this field which we must try to explore, if we are to learn anything of the most original and creative aspect of books. For this purpose, we must make do with the information supplied by statisticians who, unfortunately, have never achieved a very clear awareness of the literary phenomenon and who, even if they had appreciated it, would probably have been unable to reduce it to figures. The following pages are therefore based on a study of statistics concerning Class 8 of the Dewey decimal classification. We know already that many works which are not included in this category—history books, travel books, philosophical essays—should be considered as literary books because of the use made of them. We also know that such countries as France, Austria and the Netherlands include in Class 8 works which should normally come in Class 4 (Language) or even in other categories, provided they have some distant connection with literature. It should also be noted that, judging from their statistics, other countries such as Argentina, Greece and Pakistan apply extremely elastic criteria in regard to literature. And lastly, for a large number of countries, we do not know and probably never shall know the breakdown by categories of the books published.

In spite of all this, we can attempt to make an evaluation if we accept the hypothesis that errors cancel each other out and that, while the available figures may not be accurate, the relations between them remain significant.

Table IX shows world production, by title, of works in Class 8 for the years 1952 and 1962. For each of these years, a special column shows the percentage of the total production of the country concerned for the same year which these books represent.

The first observation suggested by this table is that literary production is stable. The total number of works in Class 8 produced throughout the world in 1952 may be estimated at 57,000 and the number of similar works produced throughout the world in 1962 at 80,000. These two figures represent precisely the same percentage—

TABLE IX

World Production (by Titles) of Works in Class 8 (Literature)
Evolution from 1952 to 1962

	1952		1962	
	Production	Percentage of Total	Production	Percentage of Total
Afghanistan	—	—	0	0
Albania	—	—	137	24
Argentina	3,258	76	1,891	57
Australia	159	25	211	12
Austria	733	23	741	21
Belgium	1,126	24	1,294	37
Brazil	870	27	716	18
Bulgaria	324	16	608 (61) or 790 (63)	16 (61) or 21 (63)
Burma	16	20	32 (60)	10
Cambodia	97 (53)	25	21	13
Cameroons	—	—	3	17
Canada	200	29	654	18
Ceylon	38	14	522	28
Chile	—	—	203	20
China (Taiwan)	—	—	1,438	55
China (Mainland)	511	20	2,851	20
Costa Rica	—	—	16	10
Cuba	70 (53)	11	156	21
Czechoslovakia	1,014	17	1,617	19
Denmark	588	27	767	18
Dominican Republic	38 (49)	33	17 (63)	24
El Salvador	—	—	20	14
Ethiopia	—	—	2	1
Finland	501	29	841	32
France	4,063	36	4,440	33
Germany (Federal Republic)	3,535	25	4,957	23
Germany (Eastern)	899 (53)	21	1,737	25
Ghana	—	—	1	0
Greece	468	31	443	35
Guatemala	25 (53)	36	37	7
Guinea	—	—	0	0
Honduras	4 (53)	6	7	4
Hungary	415 (53)	14	1,031	20

| | 1952 | | 1962 | |
	Production	Percentage of Total	Production	Percentage of Total
Iceland	133	32	194 (59)	29
India	2,467	14	3,534	32
Indonesia	100	13	97 (61)	11
Iran	202 (54)	52	211 (61)	37
Iraq	23 (53)	9	30 (59)	21
Ireland	49	33	49	23
Israel	287 (50)	35	751 (61)	30
Italy	2,979	33	2,574 (61)	35
Japan	5,650	33	5,063	23
Jordan	—	—	10 (63)	6
Kenya	—	—	4 (63)	4
Korea (Republic of)	537	39	540	15
Kuwait	—	—	6 (63)	4
Lebanon	95 (50)	24	158	39
Liberia	—	—	2 (60)	50
Libya	—	—	2 (60)	40
Luxembourg	34	8	13 (61)	10
Malaysia	—	—	9	3
Mexico	—	—	690	18
Monaco	72	70	20	53
Morocco	18	18	13 (60)	8
Netherlands	1,557	23	2,721	28
New Zealand	29	9	71	6
Nicaragua	35 (47)	29	—	—
Nigeria	—	—	12 (63)	5
Norway	752	28	898	29
Pakistan	—	—	483 (63)	21
Panama	2	9	—	—
Peru	54 (50)	7	57	7
Philippines	43 (53)	22	103 (63)	17
Poland	1,280 (55)	18	1,332	19
Portugal	314	8	913	20
Rumania	561 (53)	10	988	13
Rwanda	—	—	0	0
Saudi Arabia	—	—	55	17
Senegal	—	—	0	0
Sierra Leone	—	—	2	4
Singapore	11 (55)	23	43	18
South Africa	209	25	340 (63)	26
Spain	1,547	45	3,738	39

	1952 Production	1952 Percentage of Total	1962 Production	1962 Percentage of Total
Sudan	—	—	10 (63)	12
Sweden	1,179	36	1,772	32
Switzerland	753	23	1,263	22
Thailand	571	14	405 (61)	29
Tunisia	9 (53)	16	—	—
Turkey	409	17	805	17
Uganda	—	—	2 (63)	3
Union of Soviet Socialist Republics	5,858 (54)	12	8,083	10
United Arab Republic	122 (53)	19	465	14
United Kingdom	6,533	35	8,077	32
United States	4,423	37	7,259	33
Uruguay	16 (55)	25	68 (61) or 50 (63)	26 (61) or 36 (63)
Venezuela	106 (55)	20	51 (61) or 107 (63)	15 (61) or 14 (63)
Viet-Nam (Republic of)	213	23	171	11
Yugoslavia	1,209	23	1,659	29
Zanzibar	—	—	0	0

(Sources: *United Nations Statistical Yearbook*; R. E. Barker, *Books for All*, Unesco.)

i.e., 22·8% of world production, estimated at 250,000 in 1952 and 350,000 in 1962. A rapid glance at the above table shows that such large-scale producers of literature as the USSR, mainland China and the Federal Republic of Germany have remained reasonable stable. Others, such as the United States and the United Kingdom, have developed within relatively narrow limits. The position, however, is altogether different in the case of Japan, where the percentage of literary books dropped from 33% in 1952 to 23% in 1962, and of France, where it dropped from 36% to 33%. In the Netherlands it rose from 23% to 28%, and in Italy from 33% to 35%.

Despite the apparent stability just noted, the production of literary books over these ten consecutive years none the less displays a tendency to decline. This is shown in Diagram 1 where, on the basis of the data contained in Table IX, total production and the percentage of it represented by literary production are given side by side for about fifty countries.

DIAGRAM 1

Percentage of Literary Production in the Total Production (by Titles) for 55 Countries in 1952 and 67 Countries in 1962

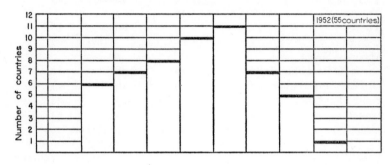

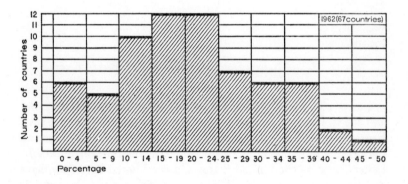

It is immediately apparent that the countries concerned form a bell-shaped curve for both 1962 and 1952; but whereas, in 1952, the mode of the curve came between twenty-five and thirty, in 1962 it came between fifteen and twenty. In other words, half the countries concerned devoted less than 20% of their production in 1962 to literary works, whereas in 1952 half of them devoted more than 25% to this type of publication. Since we have already seen that this shift does not affect the number of literary works published throughout the world, we may conclude that the proportion of such works is declining in a growing number of small-producer countries but that this decline is offset in some degree by an increase in the number of literary works in big-producer countries.

The fact is that, both as regards literary books and books in general, there are "giants" whose production exceeds 2,500 works a year. Setting aside India, for the reasons already mentioned, these countries are nine in number. In order of importance, they are the USSR, the United Kingdom, the United States, mainland China, Japan, the Federal Republic of Germany, France, Spain and Italy. These nine alone account for more than 56% of world production. In 1952, however, the figure was in the region of 60%. The decline is small but undeniable. It is due mainly to the drop, in relative terms, of Soviet production and, in absolute terms, of Japanese production. Literary production in the other countries listed is increasing.

Mention was made earlier of the influence that a given country's economic situation has on its production of functional books. Here we have, so to speak, the reverse aspect of this fact. It is obvious, for instance, that literary production in almost all the economically developing countries is relatively small. Another observation may be added to the foregoing and serves to confirm it. If, in Table IX, we take an output of 20% of literary books in 1962 as a dividing line, it will be seen that production in most Western European countries (Austria, Belgium, Finland, France, Federal Republic of Germany, Greece, Ireland, Italy, Netherlands, Norway, Spain, Switzerland and the United Kingdom) exceeds this percentage. On the other hand, production in most of the socialist countries of Eastern Europe (Czechoslovakia, Poland, Rumania, USSR) is less than 20%. Apart from Albania, which is not significant in view of its small output, the outstanding exceptions are Yugoslavia and Eastern Germany. The proportion of literary works in both countries was already above 20% in 1952 (Eastern Germany, 21%; Yugoslavia, 23%) and this trend became still more marked in 1962, where the advance was reminiscent of that in the Western countries (Eastern Germany, 25%; Yugoslavia, 29%). In the case of Yugoslavia, this was probably a consequence of the particular policy which that country has followed since 1948. The case of Eastern Germany, however, is more complex. Here it would seem that national historical factors have counted for more than political factors. In this respect, as in many others, the pattern in Eastern Germany is comparable to that in the Federal Republic of Germany. This is all the more noteworthy in that the framework of literary life is the State far more than the nation—*i.e.*, all the institutional structures which surround and govern the country's intellectual life and which set administrative limits to the book market (9). And what is striking in the case of the two Germanys is precisely the continuance of the machinery established by the unified German State prior to World War II. There will be a real divergence of pattern only if Germany's division into two States continues beyond the present literary generation.

The production and consumption of literary books are all the more closely bound up with the political structure in that these are voluntary activities reflecting a need in certain people, whether writers or readers, for communication of a certain type. This need may be restricted from outside by institutional factors—political propaganda, police, religion, etc.—or by factors acting directly, whether favourably or unfavourably, on the individual's desire and capacity for communication (illiteracy or education, poverty or high living standards). Ultimately, however, there can be no original literary production in a country unless there is a large enough number of writers to keep that production going, and a large enough number of readers to keep consumption at a level justifying that production either on doctrinal or on economic considerations. In the last resort, the popularity of literary books in the various countries thus depends, on the one hand, on a given country's political and social institutions and its inhabitants' educational level and free time and, on the other, on its demographic situation—*i.e.*, the existence of a population capable of providing simultaneously an adequate number of writers and an adequate number of readers. Neither condition is sufficient without the other. It is too often forgotten that the writer is first of all a reader, that he is a by-product of the literary environment and is supported by it not only morally but also economically. If there are not enough readers in a country to provide a livelihood for writers, then there will be fewer writers, since the only people who will be in a position to write will be those with sufficient private resources to enable them to work unpaid or, in a controlled economy, those whose livelihood is furnished by the State or some other body.

We thus come to the problem of the size of editions of literary books and, more especially, of novels, which are the most vital and characteristic examples of such works. Here, it is even more difficult than elsewhere to make evaluations. Very few countries, in their statistics, distinguish novels from other forms of literature or *belles lettres*. It is not even certain that the concept of "fiction" used in the English-speaking countries exactly corresponds with the idea of the *roman* or "novel" as used in France. For the few countries for which some information is available, the number (by titles) of novels published annually is roughly as follows:

United Kingdom	4,000 to 4,500
Federal Republic of Germany	3,000 to 3,500
United States	2,500 to 3,000
France	2,500 to 3,000
Italy	1,000 to 1,500
Spain	1,500 to 2,000

The United States may seem to occupy a modest place but in this matter as in others an upward trend is to be noted in the production of fiction which used, for preference, to take the form of magazine stories rather than novels published as books, tendencies having been radically changed by the emergence of paperbacks. Table X below clearly reveals the effect which paperbacks have had on the output of American fiction.

TABLE X

Production (by Titles) of Paperback Novels in the United States

	1961	1962	Variations
Total production of books in the United States	18,060	21,904	+21%
Total production of novels	2,630	2,942	+12%
Total production of paperback novels	1,044	1,239	+19%
Classic novels in paperbacks	603	737	+22%
Thrillers in paperbacks	248	248	0
Westerns in paperbacks	136	130	− 4%
Science fiction in paperbacks	57	124	+100%

(Source: *Publishers' Weekly*, 21 January 1963.)

Let us now consider the question of the size of literary printings—an element which is extremely difficult to pin down. In 1954, Barker boldly enough estimated the number of copies printed for each title in a few of the main categories of publications. In the case of fiction, the estimated averages were as follows:

United Kingdom	10,000
United States	8,500
Federal Republic of Germany	9,500 to 12,000
France	3,000 to 5,000
Italy	5,000 to 7,000

If we consider ordinary editions only, these figures are acceptable, and it would seem that, due allowance being made, the situation has scarcely changed since that time. This would mean that approximately 150,000,000 copies of novels are distributed annually among a readership of some 300,000,000. The ratio is not *a priori* absurd, but it must be admitted that the figures do not mean very much. It is difficult to speak of an *average* printing for a novel. Whereas for the functional book, serving a precise purpose, there can be a guaranteed minimum number of copies to be published and sold, the literary book represents a pure "adventure". Sales figures have very little to do with printing figures. Several million copies of a best-seller may be sold in a single year but in the great majority of cases, a young author's first novel, rarely published in an edition of more than 3,000, will be lucky to find a few hundred readers. It would be paradoxical to equate the tenth reprinting of a best-seller which has become a classic, or the fiftieth book by a detective-story writer whose works have enjoyed a steady success for years past, with the first book by an unknown writer or the first edition of a novel on which a well-known author has once again staked his reputation.

The most we can do is to point out that there has been a change of scale. This varies from country to country. In France, publishers are gradually making a practice of producing first editions of pocket books which run to 30,000 copies, but they seldom publish a novel on the same scale, at any rate not without having tried it out in a financially less hazardous form. In the United States, on the other hand, the risks have been affected by the progress of efficiency. Prior to the Great War, the average novel sold some 4,000 copies. After the war such best-sellers as James Cain's *The Postman Always Rings Twice* or Ernest Hemingway's *The Sun Also Rises* sold 25,000 and 30,000 respectively, while Margaret Mitchell's *Gone With The Wind* was regarded as an astonishing exception, which could never be repeated. It is none the less a fact that the ordinary edition of *Gone*

With The Wind sold a total of 5,000,000, whereas, in the United States at present, several paperback novels reach and exceed this figure every year.

At this point, we find ourselves once again confronted—but even more emphatically—with the problems that arose when we considered how mass production has taken over the publishing industry. The sudden increase in printings in the United States should not surprise or disturb us unduly. The country had leeway to make up. But we know from experience that expansion of this sort can never be confined to a single country. When an industry based on as large a population and as powerful an economy as those of the United States is set in motion, the whole balance of production and consumption throughout the world is affected. And in the case in point, what is produced and consumed is the very stuff of our culture.

NOTES

(1) R. E. Barker, *Books for All*, Unesco, 1956, p. 17.

(2) In this connection, see the admirable account published in the Unesco document, *Book Production 1937–1954 and Translations 1950–1954*, Statistical Reports and Studies, pp. 3-10.

(3) Figures provided by N. Krivenko's *Newspapers, Books, Radio and Television in the USSR*, Moscow, 1963.

(4) See above, p. 56.

(5) *Op. cit.*, p. 23. In Table 5, Barker shows the number of titles published and his own estimate of the total printing. It is therefore easy to identify the basis of his calculation.

(6) *Op. cit.*, p. 13.

(7) *Monographie de l'Edition*, 1963 edition, p. 48. The figures given for the French publishing trade's paper consumption are 48,810 tons in 1958 and 63,150 tons in 1962.

(8) Chandler B. Grannis, *What Happens in Book Publishing*, Columbia University Press, 1957, p. 8.

(9) See the author's paper presented at the IVth Congress of the International Comparative Literature Association (Freiburg, 1964): *Le cadre politique de l'histoire littéraire : peuple, classe, état ou nation.*

The Main Exchange Patterns

High- and low-pressure zones

LET us go back to the young couple of average readers discussed in the first part of this book. Allowing for differing tastes, we said, sixty or seventy books, either purchased or borrowed, enter such a household each year. These include a certain number of new works and a certain number of reprints. The proportion between the two varies considerably, depending on the countries and types of literature involved. In the case of ordinary editions of novels in France, the proportion of new works is 5 to 1, whereas, in the case of American non-fiction paperbacks, the proportion is sometimes the same in favour of reprints. Let us assume that our average couple acquires twenty new works in the course of a year—an extremely modest estimate. This means that twenty writers have worked in that year in order to meet the couple's reading requirements. A few writers produce several books a year—for instance, certain detective-story writers—but most produce at a slower rate and a substantial number produce only one book in the whole of their career. It has been estimated that the average career of an author lasts from ten to twelve years, during which he produces four to six books (1). To return to our young couple, assuming that they read twenty new books a year over a period of ten years, this implies that thirty or forty active authors are permanently working on their behalf.

It goes without saying, however, that these thirty or forty authors would die of starvation, along with their publishers, if they were to write solely for our hypothetical couple. In socialist and capitalist countries alike, all literary activity implies a minimum element of profit. It is not easy to say at what figure the number of readers becomes "economic"; this varies according to the type of book and the type of publishing involved. It may, however, be said that, on the average, a novelist in most countries would scarcely be considered to have a career unless his publisher could hope to sell at least 3,000 copies of each of his books. It may be assumed that a sale of 3,000 represents 10,000 acts of reading (2). Our thirty or forty writers must therefore have 5,000 or 6,000 couples similar to the couple described as readers of their works.

The foregoing figures are theoretical but they do highlight the fact that there is in all countries a necessary numerical relation between the book-producing and the book-consuming population. Both categories, however, form part of the total population of the country concerned and the balance between them depends on the size, the composition and the behaviour of that population.

As far as books are concerned, the number of acts of reading which take place annually in France may be estimated at 400 or 450 million. This represents a sale of 130 or 140 million copies in a reading population of 30 or 35 million. Let us assume for the time being that these 30 or 35 million people have exactly the same tastes and patterns of behaviour as those of our imaginary couple. The same thirty or forty writers will suffice to satisfy their demand, provided that the French publishing industry prints and distributes 9 or 10 million copies of each of their works. The authors to be found in the Principality of Monaco could supply the French market by themselves. If, on the other hand, each group of 10,000 French readers (since we have agreed to accept this figure as representing the level at which writing becomes economic) were to have different tastes and behaviour patterns from all the others, then this excessive diversity could be satisfied only if France possessed 150,000 active writers—in other words, more writers than there are boot- and shoe-sellers, ministers of religion and Treasury officials. With the possible exception of the United States, the USSR and China, no country in the world would number as many writers in its population. In point of fact, French literary production is the work of some 10,000 authors, of whom roughly 6,000 produce a book each year. Most of them are part-time authors of books and some 3,000 of them—*i.e.*, approximately the number belonging to the Authors' Society—are professional or semi-professional writers.

The two component elements conditioning the publication of books are therefore as follows:

1. *The existence or absence of a substantial proportion of the population which is literate, economically well off and politically influential.* This group forms the bulk of the reading public whose demand

governs literary production and, at the same time, the breeding-
ground for writers. Countries where a large literate group of this
type exists—*e.g.*, Great Britain, Germany, France, Russia and, more
recently and to a lesser extent, the United States—constitute, as it
were, literary "high-pressure zones", since the reading population
is more demanding because it is cultured and more influential because it is large. It keeps up an intense intellectual life which is
reflected in scientific, technical and political activity and in literary
or artistic creation. Meeting the needs of these groups, emerging
from this intellectual life, stimulated by the competition which it
engenders and partaking of its prestige, writers belonging to these
countries cross frontiers more easily than others.

2. *The variety or uniformity of the reading public's tastes and pat-*
terns of behaviour, regardless of the numerical importance of that
public. This may depend on many factors: the degree of intellectual
development or education, the type of political system prevailing, or
the social organization. We can obtain a very approximate, but none
the less sufficient idea of this variety by carrying out a simple calculation, made by R. E. Barker for 1952, which consists in dividing a
country's total production by titles by the number of its inhabitants (3). If the quotient is low, it means that a large number of
people are making do with a few titles and hence that there is a trend
towards uniformity. If, on the other hand, the quotient is high, it
suggests that the inhabitants of the country, even if few in number,
have a wide range of requirements. Table XI opposite compares
Barker's 1952 figures with those established by the present author in
1962 for a certain number of countries which are large or medium
producers of books.

Countries are listed in descending order of the quotients for 1962.
A trend towards standardization will be noted in the United States
and Canada, a trend which the enormous paperback printings naturally reinforced over the ten years. None the less, the pattern in both
countries (and especially Canada) has come closer to that of the
major European nations. The latter (including the USSR and various
socialist countries) lie in an intermediate zone between Italy's 162
(Italian printings being fairly large) and Portugal's 500.

It is especially noteworthy that those European countries where
the population is comparatively small but the intellectual level very
high (Switzerland, Denmark, Norway, the Netherlands, Sweden,

TABLE XI

Production (by Titles) per Million of Population

COUNTRY	*1952*	*1962*
Israel	750(50)	1,150
Switzerland	645	995
Denmark	504	893
Norway	812	857
Netherlands	673	820
Sweden	469	724
Czechoslovakia	455	628
Finland	427	587
Portugal	461	500
Austria	558	499
Hungary	341 (50)	495
United Kingdom	375	469
Rumania	158	394
Federal Republic of Germany	290	392
Belgium	512	376
Spain	119	310
Yugoslavia	305	299
France	242	270
Poland	265	237
Japan	199	231
Union of Soviet Socialist Republics*	188	195
Canada	47	193
Turkey	111	166
Italy	206	162
Argentina	237	155
United States	74	117
Mexico	114	101
China (Mainland)	5 (approx.)	38 (58)
India	47	25

(Sources: R. E. Barker, *Books For All. United Nations Statistical Yearbook. Unesco statistics.*)

* Commercially distributed books only.

Czechoslovakia, Finland etc.) have high coefficients reflecting the demands of a public which cannot be satisfied by the national output since the reservoir from which it is drawn is too small. Perhaps the most striking case is that of Israel, which has the highest quotient in the world—1,150—as might be expected in a new country which has scarcely had the time to produce writers of its own, but which has a reading public drawn from all over the world and as heterogeneous as it is intellectually active.

These countries form literary "cyclones", so to speak, attracting the production of the great anticyclones. Between these countries and the high-pressure zones described above there is an intensive exchange process, in the form of either book imports or of translations.

At the same time, there are other literary low-pressure zones which cannot be detected by means of index figures since the reading public is still too small for its demand to be reflected in local production. Such is the case of the young countries in Latin America, Africa and Asia where the birth-rate is high and where a rapid cultural development is taking place. For the present, their main need is for school-books and technical books (4), but this is only a stage. If the schools are what they should be, today's pupils will be tomorrow's individual readers. By eliminating illiteracy, by providing its people with the necessary material facilities, by subjecting them to the essential intellectual disciplines, India, for example, could create a new reading public of 300 million within the next thirty years.

How many writers would emerge from such a public? Undoubtedly, a very great number. Experience proves that there is no one-way literature and that, where reading is concerned, consumption engenders production. Countries where literary activity is most intensive—the Netherlands, for instance—are *simultaneously* high-pressure and low-pressure zones, cyclones and anticyclones, transmitters and receivers. Where they are concerned, literary exchanges are exchanges in the literal sense of the word. In respect of written culture, the same social conditions create both the supply and the demand and reading is one of those goods which are sought only when they have already been found.

International barriers

No matter what the disparities and differences between book-producing and book-consuming countries, a certain balance would eventually be established were it not that various obstacles interfere with the great exchange circuits. Some of these are natural obstacles —that is to say, they constitute part of an overall historical situation in which books are only one element—others are institutional and have been deliberately created in order to hinder the distribution of books.

The two most obvious natural obstacles are illiteracy and the diversity of languages. It would be absurd to consider these independently of each other. Since we are concerned with reading, the existence of a given language is significant only to the extent that it is read and, since we are concerned also with intercommunication, the ability to read a text in a certain language is all the more important when the language concerned is read by a large number of people.

It is generally recognized that twelve main languages are spoken by more than three-quarters of the human race. These are as follows, listed according to the percentage of the world's population which speaks them:

Chinese	25%
English	11%
Russian	8·30%
Hindi	6·25%
Spanish	6·25%
German	3·75%
Japanese	3·75%
Bengali	3·00%
Arabic	2·70%
French	2·70%
Portuguese	2·50%
Italian	2·10%

If, however, we try to determine the actual reading public in respect of each language—that is to say, the population capable of independent reading—the result will be somewhat different. An effort has been made in Table XII overleaf to determine the volume of the reading population by continent in respect of each language. For this purpose, three elements have been combined:

1. The national language or languages of each country (since two or even three national languages may coexist within one State). No allowance has been made for knowledge of foreign languages, since this factor is difficult to establish and is, in any case, of negligible importance with regard to the whole public concerned, but, on the other hand, an effort has been made to estimate the size of the peoples using a non-national language of communication—e.g., French or English in the former French or British colonies, or

TABLE XII

Reading Public classified by Language (*Units of 1,000*)

First figure: number of readers in the national language
Figure in brackets: number of readers in a second officially
recognized language of communication

LANGUAGE	AFRICA	AMERICA	ASIA	EUROPE	OCEANIA	TOTALS
English	7,500	137,300	100	40,500	9,100	194,500
	(2,800)	(3,300)	(24,200)	—	—	(30,300)
Chinese	—	—	205,500	—	—	205,500
	—	(300)	(4,100)	—	(100)	(4,500)
Russian	—	—	2,000	117,600	—	119,600
	—	—	(20,000)	(40,000)	—	(60,000)
Spanish	100	53,100	—	18,400	—	71,600
	—	(2,300)	(3,000)	—	—	(5,300)
German	—	—	—	62,000	—	62,000
	—	(300)	(100)	(100)	—	(500)
Japanese	—	—	59,700	—	—	59,700
	—	—	(2,000)	—	—	(2,000)
French	2,500	3,800	—	36,800	100	43,200
	(3,000)	—	(500)	—	—	(3,500)
Italian	—	—	—	30,300	—	30,300
	(100)	—	—	—	—	(100)
Portuguese	200	21,000	—	3,500	—	24,700
	—	—	(100)	—	—	(100)
Dutch*	3,800	—	—	12,600	—	16,400
	—	(100)	(100)	—	—	(200)
Arabic	6,300	—	1,900	—	—	8,200
	(300)	—	(500)	—	—	(800)
Indian Languages	—	—	84,000	—	—	84,000
	(300)	—	—	—	(100)	(400)
Other Asian Languages	—	—	77,500	—	—	77,500
	—	—	—	—	—	—
Non-Russian Slav Languages	—	—	—	65,800	—	65,800
	—	—	—	(2,000)	—	(2,000)
Scandinavian Languages	—	—	—	12,800	—	12,800
	—	—	—	—	—	—
Other European Languages	—	—	—	36,300	—	36,300
	—	(500)	—	—	—	(500)
African Languages	4,200	—	—	—	—	4,200
	—	—	—	—	—	—
Oceanian Languages	—	—	—	—	200	200
	—	—	—	—	—	—
Total	24,600	215,200	430,700	436,000	9,400	1,115,900
	(6,500)	(6,800)	(56,400)	(42,000)	(200)	(110,200)
Actual Population (1961)	204,000	422,000	1,721,000	648,000	17,000	3,012,000

* Including Afrikaans and Flemish.

German in areas with a high proportion of German-speaking immigrants (Israel or the American Middle West).

2. The illiteracy rate as estimated in the latest documents published by Unesco.

3. The volume of the population over fifteen years of age, this being regarded as the minimum age at which an individual is capable of independent cultural activity.

This table may be compared with that in the Unesco publication, *Basic Facts and Figures—International Statistics Relating to Education, Culture and Mass Communication* (Paris, 1958), p. 11. This latter table shows the situation in 1950. Allowance will be made for the fact that, in eleven years, the world's population increased by 20%.

Another table in the same publication (pp. 12–14) shows how various are the criteria used to evaluate illiteracy. An effort has been made to eliminate this factor in the following calculations. It seems, however, that a certain decline in illiteracy throughout the world is to be detected: in 1950, the reading population represented 36% of the world population, while in 1961 it amounted to 40%.

This table shows a language classification very different from that obtained for the spoken languages. Eight languages are sufficient for communication with three-quarters of the population of the globe, these languages being, in order of the percentages they represent, as follows:

English	18·10%
Chinese	16·9%
Russian	15·9%
Spanish	6·2%
German	5·0%
Japanese	5·0%
French	3·8%
Italian	2·4%

The reading population of the world—*i.e.*, the population not of actual readers but of individuals capable of reading independently—is estimated at 1,200 million—*i.e.*, 40% of the world population and certainly more than half of the population old enough to read.

These data might seem encouraging. If only eight main language divisions are required to cover a reading population representing two-fifths of all those over fifteen years of age and able to read anywhere in the world, the problem of communication would not seem to be insurmountable.

Unfortunately, the situation is less reassuring when we look at it more closely. To begin with, some of the most important languages of communication—Chinese, Russian, German, Japanese, Italian— are restricted to one particular part of the world. Others which, like English, Spanish or French, have spread to several continents and could be of world-wide use, are not always the most important. This applies particularly to Portuguese, Dutch and, to a lesser extent, Arabic.

The situation, moreover, varies very greatly from one continent to another. In America, for example, there is no problem. Four languages are used by a little more than 200 million people, representing half the population. These languages are virtually unchallenged, since the native American languages were not written languages in the sense which we attach to the word. The only major changes to be foreseen concern the balance between English and Spanish, as the former is at present nearing saturation point as far as the reading population is concerned while effective use of the latter, as a result of population growth and economic and social progress in Latin America, may well increase fivefold before the end of the twentieth century.

Nor is there any problem in Oceania, where the English spoken in Australia and New Zealand is unlikely to be directly challenged unless extensive political upheavals take place. The case of Africa is more complex. It is quite clear that the great colonial powers have been rather flattering themselves about their cultural achievements. The reading population using the languages of those powers represent scarcely 10% of the population of Africa, and this figure includes the whites of South Africa. Sometimes, and with some reason, French is put forward as the future language of communication in Africa. It is used either as their national language or as a secondary language by 5 or 6 million potential readers. English has more than 10 million such readers, but they are grouped in sharply defined areas and are mostly of non-African origin. Arabic, for its part, has a reading public of 7 million, but, notwithstanding the cultural support of Islam, they are limited to North Africa. French is thus, in fact, the literary language read by the largest number of native Africans over the widest area. Even if literatures should one day emerge in the indigenous African languages, it seems probable that the progress of publishing and reading in Africa will be linked to the progress made in the ability to read and write French.

There remain Asia and Europe—the two largest blocs. Three out of every eight readers in the world are Asians, three are Europeans. This equality in itself is an element of imbalance, since there are three times as many Asians as Europeans. Additionally, two-thirds of literary production throughout the world is in European languages, whereas Asian languages account for less than one-quarter. There are more than thirty written languages in Europe; in Asia there are far more, and over thirty of these are used by at least 5 million people. On the one hand, therefore, we have a very large literary production which is, however, divided among a number of languages and, on the other, we have a vast mass of potential readers, who could easily increase threefold in the decades ahead, but who are also infinitely split up by the diversity of their languages.

This would, even so, not be so very serious were it not for the fact that the linguistic division is accompanied by administrative and political division. Publication of a text in a given language does not mean that it is available to all those able to read that language. If it has the slightest ideological content, a book is unlikely to be simultaneously distributed in all the countries belonging to its own language bloc. Except in wartime, political censorship of books has been officially abolished in most countries. In actual fact, there are innumerable ways of negating this freedom from censorship. The reasons advanced for measures which prevent the distribution of a book without openly banning it are not necessarily political.

This sort of masked censorship, moreover, is not always exercised by the authorities: it may be attributable to the economic or social circles which dominate publishing in a given country.

This is a situation which will not change overnight. It is linked to the tensions and contradictions from which the modern world is suffering. Books are only a pawn in a struggle which goes far beyond literature.

This is not true, however, of the economic obstacles which confront them (5). Such obstacles are of four types:

1. Currency regulations and restrictions—an obstacle which affects both the import of books and the grant of translation rights;

2. Postal rates, an obstacle which affects all types of cultural material, newspapers, films, works of art, etc;

3. Customs regulations, involving either import licences or *ad valorem* duties;

4. Miscellaneous taxes.

A Unesco publication, *Trade Barriers to Knowledge* (Paris, 1956), reviews the very varied legal provisions existing in 92 countries. An effort had been made by the Universal Postal Union (U.P.U.) to get member countries to make systematic reductions in the postal rates applied to books and to simplify customs and administrative formalities generally. Considerable advances have been made in this direction since 1952, and some 50 States have acted on the U.P.U. recommendations. Similarly, since 1953, the International Air Transport Association has persuaded its aviation networks to extend the rate for periodicals and catalogues to books. The fact remains, none the less, that the transport of books is expensive. Even in those countries where printed-paper rates apply to books, the cost of sending a volume of average size abroad amounts to some 15 French centimes or 3 American cents. This amount may seem trifling for an individual expensive book, but it none the less has a marked effect on the price when bulk distribution of cheaper books is involved.

Any direct action in respect of currency regulations is more difficult, since each set of regulations is governed by local conditions which have nothing to do with the cultural policy followed by a given country. Unesco has done what it can to facilitate exchanges in this field by introducing international book-coupons. This system enables a Member State with a "soft" currency to obtain coupons from Unesco with which to pay for its purchases of cultural materials, these coupons being subsequently redeemed by Unesco in the currency of the supplying country. The scheme was instituted as early as 1954 and proved immediately successful among the economically developing countries.

Unesco has been trying to reduce the ill-effects of customs and financial regulations ever since its Beirut Conference in 1948, by encouraging Member States to sign agreements aimed at abolishing or lowering customs tariffs and tax charges. The basic text was adopted in 1950 by the Unesco General Conference in Florence. Under the terms of this agreement, the contracting States undertook not to apply customs duties or other charges in connection with the importation of certain items used for cultural purposes, the list being headed by printed books.

A large number of countries have signed and are applying this agreement, and we may take it that books are now circulating more or less freely among the main producer countries, more especially within the European Common Market, where the last customs duties are being removed. There is undoubtedly a general trend towards the removal of economic obstacles to the international circulation of books.

But it is precisely because of this free interchange that new problems may arise in a world where cultural inequalities and linguistic divisions are as we have outlined above. While the readership demand is developing rapidly among the peoples of Asia, Africa and Latin America, it is all too likely that this demand can be met only by the few great economic powers which have a universal language of communication or a publishing industry equipped for mass production. So far as functional books or school-books are concerned, this is not unduly serious and may even be just as well but, sooner or later, literary works rather than functional books must be considered. If they are thus to receive books "bestowed" from outside and, moreover, as far as European production is concerned, without the contribution of the minority languages, then the emerging reading public will be doomed to passivity and excluded from that active participation which distinguishes real literary life. A mediocre literature in touch with its own people is better than a good literature which is deaf to the voices of those to whom it is addressed and whose feelings and thoughts it should express.

It is precisely towards such a concentration that international exchanges are at present tending. The appearance of cheap books on the literary scene has merely accentuated this trend and facilitated the invasion of new readership areas by the output of the great powers, since cheap production is not something which can be achieved by everybody.

The international book trade

The book trade is by no means one of the major items in international economic dealings. Table XIII shows the book exports (in millions of dollars) of the main producer countries of the Western world together with the percentage of their total exports that these figures represent.

It will be seen that book exports do not account for as much as 1% of total exports in the case of any of the countries listed. Nevertheless, the volume of trade is continually increasing. If we consider book exports in terms of tonnage rather than in terms of price—an essentially variable factor—we find that they have doubled in volume in most countries over a period of ten years (6).

TABLE XIII

Main Exporters of Books (1961)

COUNTRY	Book exports (in millions) of dollars)	Percentage of exports
United Kingdom	87	0·81%
Netherlands	33	0·71%
United States	108	0·50%
France	32	0·43%
Switzerland	9	0·40%
Federal Republic of Germany	32	0·24%

The case of the Netherlands is particularly interesting. This country has a very long publishing and bookselling tradition. At a time when absolute monarchies were interfering with the flow of ideas in Europe, Dutch books in the seventeenth and eighteenth centuries provided the channel for the expression of all free thought. An intelligent policy has now made Dutch publishing one of the crossroads of scientific thought. The Netherlands receives a great deal—16% of its production consists of translations—but also gives a great deal. Between 1946 and 1961, the total value of book exports rose from 1·3 to 33 million dollars.* Even more significant is the fact that out of 7,893 titles published in 1960, 1,140 were in foreign languages and hence intended for export. This proportion of 1 in 7 is the highest of any country in the world. It means that the Netherlands, even though its national language is not, comparatively speaking, widespread, exports more books—at any rate, in value—than either France or the Federal Republic of Germany. It also means that the country has a world book market which is unique in its extent and balance:

Benelux	34·6%
Sterling area	21·5%
Federal Germany	13·5%
Dollar area	8%
France	3·9%
Netherlands possessions	3·3%
Other countries	15·2%

* Certain of these sums have been left as they appeared in the French edition —in dollars. To convert them approximately to pounds at the present rate one should, of course, divide them by 2·8.

Setting aside the special case of the Netherlands, three types of book markets are found in Western Europe:

1. *The local market*, like that of Germany, which is restricted to the Austro-Swiss bloc and a fringe of German-speaking minorities in various countries, including Poland and the United States of America.

2. *The intercontinental market*, such as that of the United Kingdom. Europe represents only a relatively small part of this. The bulk of its custom comes from the Commonwealth, its colonies, and the United States, which was itself once a colony and which, from the literary point of view at any rate, suffered from a "colonial" complex until very recently.

3. *The mixed market*, such as that of France. This combines the custom of the language bloc and that of the former colonies. French-speaking Europe (Switzerland–Benelux) almost exactly balances French possessions which have become independent, the oldest being Canada and the most recent Algeria.

Table XIII showed the United States leading the market-economy countries in the export of books. This is largely due to the policy of cultural information abroad which this country has adopted. The same obviously applies to the USSR which is not, however, included in Table XIII because of the great difficulties involved in comparing the currencies. Soviet book exports rose from 4,817,000 roubles in 1957 to 12,810,000 roubles in 1961. This latter figure represents an annual exportation of about 35 million copies (7). The United States Book Translation Programme, launched in 1950 for the purpose of distributing translations of American books to influential individuals and institutions throughout the world, and to the libraries of the American Information Services, distributed 6,593,350 volumes in 1960 (8). In comparing this with the Soviet figure, allowance must be made for the fact that such prestige exports are in addition to the trade exports which also include "programmes" sponsored by the American Federal authorities. In the years following the War, one such programme enabled "soft-currency" countries to obtain books sold in dollars. Another provides very cheap editions (between 10 and 15 cents per copy) intended for the Near East, the Far East and Africa.

An interesting coincidence which is worth noting is that the works distributed by the Book Translation Programme in 1960 were published in thirty-three different languages, while the books exported by the USSR in the same year were published in thirty-two languages other than those spoken in the Soviet Union. The similarity of the figures indicates a similarity of geographical distribution.

Nine-tenths of the books exported by the USSR are absorbed by the socialist countries. A little less than half the United States exports go to other English-speaking countries, where they have to face British competition.

For the rest, the percentage breakdown by region gives a fair idea of the areas on which the two major powers are concentrating the bulk of their efforts. Excluding other socialist countries, exports of Soviet books may be broken down as follows:

Western Europe	41%
English-speaking America	21%
Far East	16%
Latin America	6%
Near East	4%
Africa	3%
Miscellaneous	7%

The main emphasis is thus on Europe and English-speaking America. It is not surprising that, on the American side, the emphasis should be on the Far East and Latin America. Excluding the English-speaking bloc, American book exports may be broken down as follows:

Far East	33%
Latin America	27%
Europe	25%
Near East	8%
Africa	4%
Miscellaneous	8%

The size of these enormous distribution circuits is increasing from year to year. They involve both advantages and disadvantages. The advantages are especially evident in regard to the distribution of functional books in the developing countries. In almost all cases, these books are not and cannot be produced by the importing countries. But the same does not apply to literary books, which are, when all is said and done, the only medium for cultural communication. The literary book is, as we have already said, distinguished by the fact that it calls for active participation on the part of the reader. It is the reader who must stimulate production, whether local or imported.

Large-scale exports of such books under the translation pro-grammes laid down by the country of origin and in which the receiving country has no say therefore represent the main obstacle to the emergence of a genuine written culture for the masses.

This danger, moreover, has been recognized on both sides. The Soviet Union now sponsors books published outside its own fron-tiers—books which therefore represent a more direct means of main-taining contact with the consumer public.

Similarly, a conference on the development of publishing which took place in Washington in September 1964 noted in its recom-mendations that a policy of publishing development was needed in the user countries themselves and that assistance should be granted to local publishing and bookselling industries.

In any case, a genuine world book market requires the stimulus of translations made locally and in immediate contact with the reading public rather than exports and imports of printed matter.

Translations

Translations account for approximately 10% of the titles produced throughout the world. According to the *Index Translationum*, 31,384 translations were published in 1960 by forty-four countries whose total production in the same year amounted to about 310,000 titles. Allowing for the fact that many original works are translated into several languages and therefore occur several times in the list of 31,384 titles, and also that a certain number of the works—between 3 and 5% approximately—are classics translated from dead lan-guages, it is clear that translations still play only a small part as a means of international communication.

The situation is aggravated by the fact that 72 or 73% of transla-tions throughout the world are from one of the main literary lan-guages, English, Russian, French or German. This proportion has scarcely varied since 1950. English has the lion's share with 34%, Russian accounts for 16%, French for 13% and German for 10%. In the case of Russian, however, it should be noted that the figure of 16% does not have quite the same significance as the figures in respect of the other languages. So far as the latter are concerned (except in the cases of Switzerland and Belgium which are special), translation implies in principle export outside the national frontiers.

In regard to Russian, on the other hand, almost half of the translations are intended for peoples of the Soviet Union who do not use Russian as their language of communication. In order to obtain an acceptable basis for comparison in respect of international circulation, we must therefore eliminate translations from the Russian published in the Soviet Union. But this solution is not entirely satisfactory either, since the Soviet Union also exports books translated from the Russian into languages which are not spoken by any of its peoples. For this reason, the two series of figures are shown side by side in Table XIV below, which sets out the gross translation figures for forty-four countries in 1960. In the comparisons to be made hereafter, however, only the second series will be taken into account—*i.e.*, the series which leaves out translations from the Russian distributed within the Soviet Union.

TABLE XIV

Translations throughout the World

(Gross 1960 Figures for 44 Countries)

TRANSLATING COUNTRY	TOTAL	ORIGINAL LANGUAGE				
		English	Russian	French	German	Others
44 countries	31,384	10,808	4,958	3,965	3,050	8,633
USSR	5,508	663	2,289	186	298	1,820
USSR*	2,967	663	—	186	298	1,820
Germany†	2,958	1,321	323	527	4	783
Czechoslovakia	1,548	110	405	76	119	838
Italy	1,513	583	45	440	227	218
France	1,425	678	65	43	206	433
Spain	1,416	651	15	305	220	225
United States	1,294	5	168	428	286	407
Netherlands	1,269	750	29	143	220	127
Sweden	1,075	667	33	74	109	192
Japan	976	579	73	166	132	26
Belgium	874	420	17	119	177	141
Yugoslavia	849	190	88	121	122	328
Poland	803	186	172	106	100	239
Portugal	797	202	12	143	28	412
Norway	761	562	6	26	37	130
Switzerland	677	288	11	126	110	142

* Not including works translated from the Russian.
† Federal Republic of Germany and Eastern Germany.

TRANSLATING COUNTRY	TOTAL	ORIGINAL LANGUAGE				
		English	Russian	French	German	Others
Denmark	666	355	14	57	73	167
India	618	262	47	28	14	265
Finland	618	298	17	36	77	190
Rumania	595	26	247	26	34	262
Bulgaria	548	24	296	19	31	178
Israel	532	237	21	38	52	184
Brazil	464	210	19	120	35	80
Argentina	421	203	10	77	55	76
United Kingdom	411	7	15	126	69	194
Turkey	400	151	17	85	41	106
Hungary	398	64	119	69	71	75
UAR	306	234	11	31	6	24
Korea (Republic of)	233	147	10	28	30	18
Greece	192	107	18	44	11	12
Mexico	173	116	5	17	9	26
Iceland	134	50	2	10	18	54
Ceylon	110	58	8	3	0	41
Albania	108	2	20	8	5	25
Austria	103	62	3	22	0	16
Iran	102	79	3	4	3	26
China (Taiwan)	100	83	2	8	3	4
Canada	53	29	0	8	2	14
South Africa	52	28	0	4	7	13
Indonesia	50	18	2	1	2	27
Viet-Nam (Republic of)	49	22	0	25	2	4
Chile	42	16	3	8	4	9
Burma	35	27	0	2	0	6
Pakistan	29	24	0	0	0	5

The translating countries have been listed in the above table in order of importance, beginning with those which publish the largest number of translations. It will be observed that, even when works translated from the Russian are excluded, the Soviet Union still heads the list, immediately followed, it is true, by Germany, or, more precisely, the two Germanys, since the translation statistics make no distinction between them.

The main currents of exchange may be seen at a glance. The most important is from the English area in the direction of Germany (1,321 titles), with the English flow towards the Netherlands, France, the USSR, Sweden, Spain, Italy and Norway coming well behind and being of very similar importance (750 to 562). Then comes a fairly wide gulf between this group and Belgium's 420.

It is at roughly this level that the French currents begin, the most important being the Franco-German (527), followed by the Franco-Italian (440), the Franco-American (428) and, trailing far behind, the Franco-Spanish (305). The outflow from Russian naturally goes in the first instance to the socialist countries, extending from 405 in the case of Czechoslovakia to 119 in the case of Hungary, although Germany is still a good customer with 323, as is the United States with 168. The German currents are more diffused and distributed more evenly—the USSR and the United States are roughly at the same level, and Italy, Spain, the Netherlands and France come between 298 and 206.

It will be observed that only a few translations are published in the United Kingdom, although this country is the second largest exporter of books in the world. This indicates, up to a certain point, that translations may be regarded as complementary to the book export trade. Within this language bloc, where production is high and a large number of customers exists, there is no necessity to call on outside production: books in English are exported from one English-speaking country to another and are exported primarily from Britain. The United Kingdom is the perfect example of what we have called a "literary anticyclone". Currents go out from it but are not drawn into it. This self-sufficiency results from the strength of the British book market, but as far as the future is concerned, is also one of the great weaknesses of English literature.

The fact that certain countries attract translations while others resist them becomes evident when, instead of the gross figures, we consider the figures in relation to national production. What is the proportion of translations in each country in relation to the total production of books? We have already seen that the world average was 10%, but there are very considerable variations from this average, as may be seen from Table XV.

One thing is immediately apparent from this table. As already pointed out, the world average is in the region of 10%, and it is here that we find such countries as France and Germany, where the pattern, generally speaking, is close to that of the world average. But twenty-six countries are above the average while only eighteen are below. This imbalance clearly demonstrates that the countries

TABLE XV

The Proportion of Translations

Percentage of translations in relation to national production (1960)

LARGE TRANSLATORS		AVERAGE TRANSLATORS		SMALL TRANSLATORS	
Country	%	*Country*	%	*Country*	%
Israel	34·0	Italy	19·7	Rumania	9·4
Albania	25·5	Denmark	18·9	Brazil	9·4
Finland	24·8	Iceland	18·9	Mexico	8·8
Belgium	23·9	Sweden	18·5	United States	8·6
Norway	23·3	Iran	17·9	Hungary	7·6
Spain	23·3	Czechoslovakia	17·0	China (Taiwan)	6·3
		Bulgaria	16·3	Ceylon	6·2
		Netherlands	16·1	India	5·8
		Yugoslavia	15·8	Viet-Nam	
		Korea		(Republic of)	5·0
		(Republic of)	14·4	Pakistan	4·8
		Switzerland	13·8	Indonesia	4·5
		UAR	13·3	Japan	4·1
		Greece	12·2	USSR†	4·0
		Portugal	12·0	Austria	3·0
		Turkey	11·6	Chile	2·7
		France	11·2	South Africa	2·0
		Poland	11·0	Canada	1·9
		Germany*	10·9	United Kingdom	1·7
		Burma	10·6		
		Argentina	10·4		

* Federal Republic of Germany and Eastern Germany.

† Not including works translated from Russian into another Soviet language.

below the average are those with the highest production, and these include the United States, Japan, the USSR and—the furthest below of all—the United Kingdom. This provides a striking confirmation of the fact that the higher a country's production, the less need that country has of a contribution from outside. This is one of the least obvious but most serious dangers that material and intellectual strength can entail for the culture of a great country.

Unless precautions are taken for the systematic maintenance of links with other countries, there is reason to fear the consequences of cultural inbreeding. It is not only the underdeveloped countries which need a strict publishing policy.

However this may be, the main translator countries are headed by those "low-pressure areas" mentioned above—first and foremost, Israel, followed by Finland, Belgium and Norway (Denmark, Iceland, Sweden and the Netherlands come fairly close behind, among the average translators). We also have the other type of translator country, such as Albania or Spain, which, because of temporary historical circumstances (very different in the two cases), is not in a position to produce at a level high enough to meet its demand.

In the face of this imbalance, it may be asked to what extent the translator countries are tributary to the large producer countries. Table XIV showed the dominant currents of translation in absolute terms. It will be interesting to consider them also in relative terms— *i.e.*, to see what proportion of translations in each country are drawn from one or another language. An attempt has been made to establish this in Table XVI, where the countries are classified according to the

TABLE XVI

Dominant Translation Trends—Dominant Languages in 1960

Percentage of translations in each translator country for each original language

COUNTRY	ORIGINAL LANGUAGES				
	English	Russian	French	German	Miscel-laneous
A. *Dominant language : English*					
1. *Only dominant language*					
Pakistan	83	—	—	—	17
2. *Plus Russian dominant*					
Ceylon	52	7	3	—	38
India	42	8	5	2	43
Indonesia	36	4	2	4	54
Poland	23	21	13	13	30
3. *Plus French dominant*					
China (Taiwan)	83	2	8	3	4
Iran	78	3	4	3	12
Burma	77	—	6	—	17
UAR	77	4	10	2	7
Mexico	67	3	10	5	15
Austria	60	3	21	—	16
Japan	59	8	17	14	2
Greece	56	9	23	6	6

	English	Russian	French	German	Miscellaneous
Canada	55	—	15	—	30
Argentina	48	2	18	13	19
Spain	46	1	22	16	15
Brazil	45	4	26	8	17
Germany*	45	11	18	—	26
Switzerland	43	2	19	16	20
Italy	39	3	29	15	14
Chile	38	7	19	14	22
Turkey	38	4	21	10	27
Portugal	25	2	18	4	49
Yugoslavia	22	10	14	14	40
4. Plus German dominant°					
Norway	74	1	4	5	16
Korea (Republic of)	63	4	12	13	7
Sweden	62	3	7	10	18
Netherlands	59	2	11	17	13
South Africa	54	—	8	13	25
Denmark	53	2	9	11	25
Belgium	48	2	14	20	16
Finland	48	3	6	12	31
France	48	5	3	15	29
Israel	45	4	7	8	36
Iceland	37	2	8	13	40
USSR†	22	—	6	10	62
B. Dominant language : Russian					
1. Plus French dominant					
Albania	6	61	7	5	21
2. Plus German dominant					
Bulgaria	4	54	3	6	33
Rumania	4	42	4	6	44
Hungary	16	30	17	18	19
Czechoslovakia	7	25	5	8	54
C. Dominant language : French					
1. Plus English dominant					
Viet-Nam (Republic of)	45	—	51	4	—
2. Plus German dominant					
United States	—	13	33	22	32
United Kingdom	2	4	31	17	46

* Federal Republic of Germany and Eastern Germany.
° See also A.2 Indonesia and A.3 Yugoslavia.
† Not including works translated from Russian into another Soviet language.

dominant language and then reclassified within the resulting groups according to the second dominant language.

Quite clearly, only English and Russian can truly claim to be primary dominant languages. French dominates in only three countries, two of which are the great English-language producers—namely, the United States and the United Kingdom, where English obviously cannot be a source of translation and hence does not compete with other languages. The third country is the former French colony of the Republic of Viet-Nam.

The position of French is none the less still strong, since the most frequent combination is English as the first dominant language, with French as the second. Such is the case of eighteen countries out of forty-four. Among these countries, the cases of Germany and Austria in regard to translations from the German is similar to that of the United Kingdom and the United States in regard to translations from the English, in that German is the national language and therefore cannot compete with other languages as a translation source. The same applies to France, where German is the second dominant language, since French, as the national language, cannot compete with German. This being said, it will be observed that those countries which combine English and French are, first of all, the countries of Southern Europe (Greece, Spain, Italy and Portugal), together with the Middle Eastern countries (Iran, UAR and Turkey), the Latin American countries (Mexico, Argentina, Brazil and Chile) and certain Far Eastern countries (China (Taiwan), Burma and Japan). The case of Canada is too obvious to require comment.

While the English–French combination is found in eighteen countries, English–German is found in twelve. Most of these are Northern European countries with a Germanic rather than a Latin tradition. To these should be added Israel, where, however, French is almost on the same footing as German.

The English–Russian combination is found in five countries, three being relatively underdeveloped Far Eastern countries (Ceylon, India and Indonesia) and two European people's democracies (Poland and Yugoslavia). Similarly, people's democracies appear among the countries—five in number—where Russian is the main dominant language. Russian is most frequently linked with German (Bulgaria, Rumania, Hungary and Czechoslovakia) since the latter has always been one of the main languages used for the communication of Marxist thought. French is the second dominant language only in the case of Albania, a fact which is not surprising since most of the Albanian leaders are French-speaking.

Another question arising is that of the nature of the translations. We know that the place held by literature in the production of the various countries differs very greatly. The same applies to translations. A country may be primarily interested in obtaining literature from another country or, alternatively, may be primarily interested in obtaining scientific information. Table XVII embodies three lists, each of them representing a regrouping of the decimal classification categories. The first concerns translations of a literary nature, the second those relating to the social sciences (history, sociology, demography, human geography, economics, etc.), and the third works in the pure and applied sciences. In each list, the countries are arranged in decreasing order of the importance they attach to the category concerned. Thus, 84% of the translations made in Iceland consist of literary works, whereas only 14% of those in Indonesia belong to that category. Conversely, 70% of Indonesia's translations relate to the social sciences, as against only 13% of Hungary's. It will be observed that three columns, numbered 1, 2 and 3, follow each of the percentage columns. Column 1 refers to "literary low-pressure" countries—*i.e.*, with a high cultural level and hence a high demand, but a numerically small population and a small distribution area for the language. There are six such countries, each of them indicated by a cross. Column 2 relates to the seven English-speaking countries on the list, whether English is the main or only the secondary language. Finally, column 3 refers to the eight countries of the European socialist bloc. This arrangement will enable us to examine the relation between each of these three very different factors and the dominant interests in translation.

It is obvious that the "literary low-pressure" countries confirm the hypothesis we made about them. It will be seen that they are all grouped together at the head of the "literature" list. So far as these countries are concerned, translations represent first and foremost a supplement to the literary material available. None of them devotes less than three-quarters of its translation activities to literature. On the other hand, the same countries, which have highly developed university systems, are less dependent on foreign production in respect of the social sciences and occupy a position at the foot of the social science list which is absolutely symmetrical with their position at the head of the literary list. None of them devotes

TABLE XVII

Dominant Translation Trends—Types of Works dominating in 1960

LITERATURE					SOCIAL SCIENCES				
Country	%	1	2	3	*Country*	%	1	2	3
Iceland	84	+			Indonesia	70			
Norway	81	+			United Kingdom	63	+		
Portugal	81				Iran	58			
Hungary	77			+	Burma	51			
Denmark	75	+			UAR	50			
Sweden	75	+			Argentina	46			
Austria	74				Pakistan	45	+		
Netherlands	74	+			United States	44	+		
Finland	73	+			Brazil	43			
Canada	72		+		India	42	+		
Albania	71			+	Ceylon	41	+		
Greece	69				Chile	40			
Germany	66				South Africa	39	+		
Belgium	65				China (Taiwan)	37			
Viet-Nam (Republic of)	63				Mexico	35			
Turkey	63				Spain	35			
Yugoslavia	62			+	Bulgaria	34			+
France	62				Israel	34			
Israel	60				Switzerland	34			
South Korea	59				Italy	33			
Italy	57				Japan	33			
Switzerland	56				Viet-Nam (Republic of)	33			
Czechoslovakia	55			+	Korea (Republic of)	31			
Chile	55				France	30			
USSR	54			+	Poland	28			+
Poland	53			+	Yugoslavia	28			+
Japan	51				Rumania	27			+
Spain	51				Albania	26			+
China (Taiwan)	51				Belgium	26			
India	50	+			Canada	26		+	
Rumania	48		+		Germany	26			
Ceylon	46	+			Greece	26			
Brazil	44				USSR	26			+
South Africa	44	+			Austria	24			
UAR	42				Czechoslovakia	22			+
Argentina	40				Turkey	22			
United States	40	+							

Country	%	1	2	3
Burma	37			
Bulgaria	37	+		
Mexico	36			
United Kingdom	30	+		
Iran	23			
Pakistan	17	+		
Indonesia	14			
Denmark	20	+		
Netherlands	20	+		
Portugal	18			
Finland	18	+		
Sweden	16	+		
Norway	15	+		
Iceland	14	+		
Hungary	13			+

PURE AND APPLIED SCIENCES

Country	%	1	2	3
Pakistan	38	+		
Bulgaria	29		+	
Mexico	29			
Rumania	25		+	
Czechoslovakia	23		+	
USSR	20		+	
Poland	19		+	
Iran	18			
South Africa	17	+		
United States	16	+		
Indonesia	16			
Japan	15			
Turkey	15			
Spain	14			
Argentina	14			
Brazil	13			
Ceylon	13	+		
Burma	12			
China (Taiwan)	12			
Hungary	10		+	
Italy	10			
South Korea	10			
Switzerland	10			
Yugoslavia	10			+
Belgium	9			
Finland	9	+		
Sweden	9	+		
France	8			
Germany	8			
India	8		+	
UAR	8			
United Kingdom	7	+		
Israel	6			
Netherlands	6	+		
Chile	5			
Denmark	5	+		
Greece	5			
Norway	4	+		
Viet-Nam (Republic of)	4			
Albania	3			+
Canada	3		+	
Austria	2			
Iceland	2	+		
Portugal	1			

more than 20% of its translation activity to these sciences. As regards pure science, the trend is the same as in the case of the social sciences, although it is not perhaps quite so clear-cut. Although the six countries come at the foot of the list, they are not grouped together to the same extent as in the previous column. The reason for this difference is probably that the production of original social science books calls mainly for social scientists, whereas the production of books dealing with the pure and applied sciences calls for technical installations which are not always within the reach of countries with a small population, however rich those countries may be.

A comparable symmetry is apparent in the case of the English-speaking countries, but the general trends are less clear-cut. Canada, in particular, displays a pattern which deviates from that of the other countries in its language bloc and comes closer to that of the countries in column 1. The other English-speaking countries do not translate many literary works, a fact which confirms the belief that the insularity of English is indeed of a literary kind. On the other hand, the same countries are extensive translators of social science publications, although membership of the English-language bloc is apparently not a factor of distinction in respect of the pure and applied sciences. In this branch, the United States and the United Kingdom, which have similar patterns for literature and the social sciences, differ very greatly from each other. It is probably because of the development of atomic and space research in the United States that this country is more receptive than others to foreign scientific production.

As far as membership of the group of European socialist countries is concerned, this would not seem to constitute a factor of distinction in regard to literature. In Hungary, literature represents 77% of all translations as compared with 37% in Bulgaria. The socialist countries, however, display a common attitude towards functional books. All of them are medium or moderate translators of the social sciences, the proportion being between 13% and 34%. This is perhaps attributable to the fact that, in a field which is closely connected with their fundamental doctrine, these countries translate mainly within their bloc and, more especially, from the Russian. It might, however, be remarked that while this would not apply to the pure and applied sciences category, the percentage of all translations is in this case only between 3% and 25%, for these countries.

All the foregoing shows that translation plays a very localized and, above all, a very specialized role in international literary exchanges. Moreover, we have so far considered only the four main languages. Where the others are concerned, the part played by translation is virtually non-existent. In Italy, for example, between 2,000 and 2,500 literary works are published annually. Less than five of these are at all likely to be translated in the United States and less than three in the United Kingdom. In other words, the distribution of Italian literature in the two great English-speaking consumer countries is negligible, even though Italian is the language of a European country. If we now turn to Chinese, for example, we find that all the translations made in Western Europe and the United States together amount to barely one half of one thousandth of one of the richest productions in the world. This is not due to political considerations, since Japanese is just as badly placed: the total number of translations from the Japanese varies within a given period between 1·2 and 1·5 for every thousand translations made throughout the world, and literature accounts for only half of this figure. Yet Japanese literature at present represents between 4% and 5% of the world's output.

There are many reasons for this situation. So far, attention has been concentrated mainly on the problem of international copyright, which involves the same institutional barriers which hinder the free circulation of books. Additionally, the system for paying authors varies greatly from one country to another, and the protection of literary property after the author's death likewise varies to a considerable extent. As early as 1886, forty-six countries, most of them European, and including the United Kingdom, France and the British and French possessions, accepted the Berne Convention, Article 4 of which stipulates that "authors who are subjects or citizens of any of the countries of the Union shall enjoy in countries other than the country of origin of the work, for their works, whether unpublished or first published in a country of the Union, the rights which the respective laws do now or may hereafter grant to natives."

Article 2 of the Universal Copyright Convention, concluded in Geneva in 1952 as a result of Unesco's efforts, embodies a similar position but carries protection still further. This convention has so far been signed by forty-five countries, most of them already signatories to the Berne Convention.

It should be added that the pirating of books, which consists of translating a work without paying royalties, is still very common. This is regrettable both morally and economically, yet it must be recognized that elimination of this clandestine market would reduce exchanges still further. It exists mainly in those countries where the currency is too "soft" or the market too small for publishers to be able to add the payment of substantial royalties to their other costs.

The real obstacle to translation is therefore the problem of investment arising from the particular costs of this type of publication. If we agree that the smaller the market, the larger a publisher's profit margin should be, it is obviously difficult for a small country to indulge in publishing ventures where to the residual rights of the original publisher and the author must be added the translator's.

The translation market is unlikely to develop in the near future since its shortcomings are precisely those of international life in the modern world. It is true that it has the benefit of certain technical advances, more especially in the sphere of communications. The time for translation has considerably decreased over the last few hundred years. In the days of *Don Quixote*, it took fifty years for a book to circulate throughout Europe, whereas now books are commonly translated within a year of their original publication. This apart, however, the situation is basically the same as it was when printing first began. Translation is not an extension of publication but is superimposed on it and introduces a new complexity into the already cumbersome machinery.

Books undergo their first test within a certain literary market, language bloc, ideological bloc or State. Where a book fails this test, there is no longer any question of translating it even though, in other countries, there may be an unsuspected public eager to welcome it. If it has some success, options will be taken on it, but will hardly ever be implemented and the book will undergo a second process of selection, made haphazard on the basis of superficial readings. This selection is all the more severe in that it is gratuitous and without any sound sociological groundwork: very few people are capable of appraising a book in one language and predicting the effect it will have, when translated, on a public speaking another language.

Hence, even if the book is accepted by a foreign publisher, it must run all the risks involved in a second venture, with the translator's involvement added to that of the author, sometimes with disastrous results. The venture, moreover, is all the less tempting in that the financial risks are increased because of the number of parties concerned. Translated books must compete with books published in their original language. It is difficult to increase a margin of profit which must provide for payment to the author, the original publisher, the second publisher and the translator. Generally speaking, it is the latter who suffers—which is a mistake, since good translations are in fact rewritings and the ideal translator should be at least as talented as the author he is translating.

Since translators are mostly mediocre and poorly paid, it is by no means certain that the enterprise will be a literary success even if it proves financially advantageous. Works in translation are offered to a public for which they were not originally designed, a public which did not demand them, which did not seek them; they are sent forth in garments which are not their own nor those of which the new readers dreamed, and they are therefore deprived of that capacity for dialogue which is basic to literary life. The most that can be hoped for is that the book will at least be "deformed" to some purpose, that it will serve, as Kipling said, "to uphold or to embellish same ancient truth restated, or some old delight returned" (9). It would be a mistake to neglect the contribution made by such "creative treason" (10), to which so many works owe their survival and even a sort of immortality, but it can scarcely be accepted as a rule and still less as the basis for a translation policy.

If there is any solution to the problem it may perhaps be found in mass publication, which cannot make do with unduly narrow distribution areas. The huge printings involved mean that linguistic boundaries must be overstepped and the heavy investments made in such publishing provide the means to achieve this. Continental Europe and Asia, each in its own way, may find a solution to their multilingual problem in one or more "common translation markets".

The system of translations within the USSR may provide a source of inspiration, if not a model. Fifty out of every hundred works translated into Russian were originally published in other Soviet Union languages and fifty in foreign languages. Out of every hundred works translated into the various non-Russian languages of the Soviet Union, five were originally published in one of those languages, eighty in Russian and fifteen in a foreign language. Out of every hundred works translated into foreign languages, ninety were originally published in Russian, between six and eight in a non-Russian language of the Soviet Union, and the remainder in a foreign language. It is true that Russian accounts for the bulk of these exchanges, but this is justified by the overwhelming numerical superiority of Russian-speaking people in the USSR, while, in any case, the volume and variety of the exchanges are very much greater than any to be found elsewhere in the world.

A few tentative but successful efforts (11) suggest that a similar policy might be established between European countries which do not have a universal language. It would be sufficient to regard publication of a book from the outset as being designed for several countries. The books to be published could be selected on the basis of the global requirements of a public drawn from several nationalities. At the very beginning, the author would collaborate with his translators, guiding and perhaps being guided by them. While the artist's fiat may remain an individual thing, there is none the less a stage in the process of literary composition which can be carried out by a team. When the time came to manufacture the book, it would already have several different faces, all of them similar; it would have several voices, all of them authentic; and it would already have over-come the language barrier. Just as the author's royalties would be included in the fees paid to the team, so the cost of each national edition would be included in the overall calculations for the financial undertaking.

In terms of paperbacks, conceived on the scale now found in the United States, the increase in costs would have only a minimal effect on the retail price per copy and, in any case, the translated editions would be more profitable than at present.

The above paragraphs are in the subjunctive, but could certainly be put into the indicative at some future stage. Undertakings of this kind will become practical propositions only when the revolution in the book world has made itself felt in the hearts and minds of men. From one end to another of the chain, author, publisher, bookseller, librarian and even individual readers must consent to undergo the radical change which books themselves have already undergone.

NOTES

(1) See David T. Pottinger, *The French Book Trade in the Ancien Régime*, *op. cit.*, and my own article, also quoted previously, *La problème de l'âge dans la productivité littéraire*.

(2) The generally accepted figure of 3·5 readers for 1 purchaser was confirmed by all surveys. The expression 'act of reading' is used to mean reading by an individual of an individually acquired text.

(3) R. E. Barker, *op. cit.*, p. 21, Table 3.

(4) School and technical books at present account for 90% of consump-tion in the economically developing countries (Conference on the role of books in economic and social development, Washington, 11–15 September 1964).

(5) In regard to the questions dealt with in the following pages, see the Unesco pamphlet *Trade Barriers to Knowledge*, revised edition, 1956.

(6) *La Monographie de l'Edition*, published by the Syndicat National des Editeurs Français, on p. 83 of the 1963 edition, gives figures which

differ slightly from ours but are of the same order (United Kingdom: 0·8%; United States: 0·4%; France: 0·59%; Federal Germany: 0·26%).

(7) *Book Publishing in the USSR*, American Book Publishers Council, New York, 1963, pp. 39–43. This is the report of a delegation of American publishers who visited the USSR in 1962. The figures are given in 'heavy' 1962 roubles.

(8) Report by Mr Warren M. Robbins, of the United States State Department, on the role of publishing in cultural development (typed Unesco document).

(9) Address to the Royal Society of Literature, 1926.

(10) See R. Escarpit, *"Creative treason" as a Key to Literature. Yearbook of Comparative and General Literature*, Bloomington, Indiana, No. 10, 1961.

(11) *E.g.*, the joint publication by Sythoff of Leyden and Heinemann of London of Netherlands novels in Dutch and in English, in the 'Bibliotheca Neerlandica' series, with the assistance of the Prince Bernhard Foundation. By mid-1965, eight major publishers announced they had formed a group for the co-publication of books in seven languages. They belonged to the following countries: U.S.A., United Kingdom, Sweden, France, the Netherlands, Germany, Italy, Spain. The first five books were to appear in February 1966.

PART THREE

Future Prospects

The Publishing Dilemma

Immediate popular successes and steady-sellers

IN a famous passage in his *Lettre sur le commerce de la librairie*,
Diderot wrote, "A folly continually committed by those who let
themselves be ruled by general theories consists in applying the
principles of cloth manufacture to the publication of books. These
people reason as though publishers could manufacture in strict proportion to their sales and the only risks involved lay in eccentric
tastes and changing fashions; they overlook or are unaware—which
they may indeed be—that it would be impossible to sell a book at a
reasonable price without producing a sufficient number of copies
of it. What remains of an old-fashioned material in the mercers'
warehouses is still of some value; what remains of a poor book in a
publisher's stocks is of none. To this must be added the fact that,
out of every ten ventures, one is successful—and this is already a
great deal—four make ends meet in the long run, and five show a
final loss." (1)

This text dates from June 1767. Two hundred years later, notwithstanding all the changes that have occurred both in publishing
techniques and in the structure of the reading publics, it remains
essentially true. Let us concentrate on the final observation concerning publishing ventures. Diderot distinguishes three types of books:
those which are immediately successful, those which succeed "in the
long run", and those which fail. He considers that the proportion
of failures is the measure of the commercial hazard that publishers
have to face. In this particular regard, the situation is probably
somewhat different nowadays. Publishing houses have become large
firms with huge capital resources which enable them to spread the
risk over a large number of operations.

It is none the less true that a book is a failure if the publisher loses
all or part of the money he puts up, and that it is a success if the

publisher not only recovers his investment but also makes a more or less substantial profit. Moreover, modern publishers, like Diderot himself, consider that there are two sorts of successes—a "cash-down" success, where a book brings in returns very quickly in a single operation without any further tying-up of capital, and a "long-term" success, which calls for a long-range policy during which the capital involved and even all or part of the profit are hazarded several times over.

There are, therefore, several forms of success. "Fast-sellers" very rapidly achieve high sales, pay for themselves within a few weeks and then gradually drift into oblivion without there being any need to tie up fresh capital for reprints. "Steady-sellers" start slowly but evenly and their sales are subject only to seasonal variations occasioned by holidays, the beginning of the school year, literary prizes, gift seasons, etc. These books pay for themselves over a period of months or even years, but their enduring popularity enables the publisher to reinvest his capital several times over without any danger. Finally, best-sellers represent the most spectacular type of success, since they combine both sorts of sales—beginning as fast-sellers, they end up as steady-sellers.

The curves in Diagram 2 illustrate these three types of successes(2). The months are shown along the axis of abscissas, and monthly sales, estimated as a percentage of the minimum quantity of copies which must be sold to ensure a profit, are given as the ordinates. In actual fact, publishers do not know the exact sales figures, at any rate in the months immediately following publication. They only know the re-stocking figures—*i.e.*, the orders placed by bookshops after the copies they hold on a sale or return basis, or previously purchased by them, have been sold. It is only when unsold copies are returned after several months that the real sales can be evaluated. Nevertheless, if we accept the hypothesis that any re-order represents the sale of at least one copy, we can obtain a fair idea of the rate of sales. The main thing is to be able to forecast the situation with sufficient accuracy to decide in good time whether the book in question should be reprinted or not. An over-evaluation of sales may leave the publisher with unsold stocks on hand which will eat up, and more than eat up, his profits. Miscalculation in the other direction is liable to break the flow of sales by interrupting supplies to booksellers while reprinting, decided on too late, is hastily carried out.

The following examples are based on actual cases, but distortion due to the individual features of the works concerned have been eliminated so as to make these cases more representative.

DIAGRAM 2

Restocking Curves

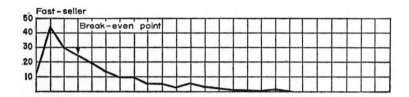

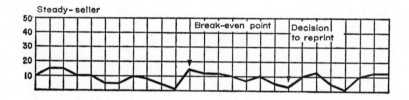

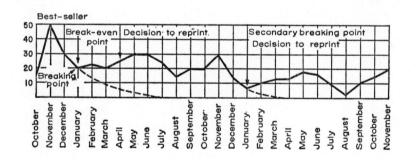

In the case of the fast-seller, the curve is a simple one. After a time-lag, which may vary in duration but which seldom exceeds three weeks, sales begin and rise immediately to their maximum level. Thereafter, they tend to diminish steadily in line with a curve which is recognizably a hyperbola of the function $x = \dfrac{a}{y}$. If the fore-

casts have been accurate, sales will drop to practically nothing just before the initial stocks are exhausted, so that there will be no occasion to reprint.

The curve in respect of the steady-seller is quite different. Sales figures do not soar sharply at an early date, but maintain a regular level and seasonal variations recur in roughly the same form each year. It is therefore relatively easy for the publisher to make his forecasts. Profits are slow, but the decision to reprint can be taken without undue risk once a certain stage has been passed—*e.g.*, when stock in hand is less than sales over the preceding financial year.

The best-seller curve combines the features of both the fast-seller and the steady-seller. A best-seller is in fact a fast-seller which, at a certain point, develops into a steady seller while still retaining certain features of its original sales pattern. It starts like an ordinary success: a time-lag followed by a peak and then by the beginning of

a decline in line with a hyperbola of function $x = \dfrac{a}{y}$. At a certain point,

however, the descending curve is interrupted and starts to follow the movement of that of a steady-seller. Many publishers fail to appreciate the significance of this break in the curve and are taken unawares by the sudden change in the pattern. It is true that it is very difficult to make forecasts in respect of best-sellers since, as will be seen later, best-sellers are books which break out of the social circle for which they were originally intended. Sales show the same seasonal variations as in the case of the steady-seller, but, from time to time, there are seemingly unaccountable upward movements when the best-seller penetrates a hitherto untouched social group. The pattern is then the same as in the case of the book's original launching. Sales rocket, sometimes higher than at the time of the initial spurt, and this is followed by the beginning of a descending hyperbola. If the book is destined for lasting success, a secondary breaking-point is then found, reintroducing the pattern of the steady-selling book.

The three types of curves seldom occur in their pure form. The typical steady-seller is almost always a functional book which meets a continuing need—*e.g.*, a school textbook, a scientific treatise or, an even better example from the stability angle, a cookery book.

Successful literary books generally have the transitory quality of the fast-seller. Best-sellers are extremely rare and represent barely 2 or 3% of successful books. Even so, it must be clearly understood that the best-seller is determined not by the number of copies sold but by the type of sales pattern, in other words by the combination of an initial peak and a descending hyperbola interrupted at the breaking-point when the book's sales level off. A book may be a best-seller with a sale of 50,000 just as much as with a sale of 3,000,000.

Very few books have a long life. Out of a hundred works published, scarcely ten still sell a year later, and ten times fewer twenty years later. A confirmation of this may be found in the fact that the number of titles available for sale in a given country amounts to about ten times the average yearly production.

This rapid attrition in literary production has been highlighted by Hans Ferdinand Schulz in his book *Das Schicksal der Bücher und der Buchhandel* (3). His method consisted in examining successive re-issues in relation to German literary production between 1950 and 1958. It can be seen at once that, on the average, second editions represent roughly 10% of first editions, that eighth editions represent 1% and that twenty-fifth editions represent 0·1%. "Edition" is taken here as meaning not only new publications of the same text by the same or another publisher, but also successive re-impressions of a given work using the same plates. It will therefore be seen that there is only one impression where the overwhelming majority of books published in the Federal Republic of Germany is concerned. These are either failures from the bookseller's point of view or books of the fast-seller type.

It is of particular interest to check the hypothesis put forward earlier when we identified popular successes with literary books and steady sellers with functional books. Hans Ferdinand Schulz provided separate figures for the various types. Table XVIII reproduces those relating to literary books, on the one hand, and to school-books, on the other. In order to facilitate comparison, the first column, for each type, gives the gross figures while the second shows how many these figures represent per 1,000 first editions.

It is clear that literary books decline much more rapidly than school-books.

In fact, two entirely different types of publishing are involved. It is not the different features of their form or their aesthetic merits which determine whether books belong to the category of popular successes or steady sellers, but the very structure of the publishing

TABLE XVIII

Reissues in the Federal Republic of Germany between 1950 and 1958

EDITIONS	LITERARY BOOKS		SCHOOL-BOOKS	
	Gross Figures	per 1,000	Gross Figures	per 1,000
1st	24,455	1,000·0	8,462	1,000·0
2nd	2,403	98·3	2,677	316·4
3rd	732	29·9	1,404	165·9
4th	471	19·3	1,074	126·7
5th	334	13·7	825	97·5
6th	272	11·2	664	78·5
7th	188	7·7	505	59·6
8th	146	6·0	389	46·0
9th	142	5·8	288	34·0
10th	102	4·2	217	25·6
11th	82	3·4	168	19·8
12th	66	2·7	124	14·7
13th	59	2·4	87	10·3
14th	63	2·6	81	9·6
15th	61	2·5	73	8·6
16th	54	2·2	71	8·4
17th	47	1·9	55	6·5
18th	35	1·4	54	6·4
19th	37	1·5	49	5·8
20th	45	1·8	47	5·6

(Source: Hans Ferdinand Schulz.)

process as deliberately laid down by the publisher, having regard to the type of work which he is distributing and the type of public at which he is aiming.

Programmed publication and non-programmed publication

To convey the concept of publication most languages use one of two metaphors which are contained in the Latin word *edere* (*ex dare*) and *publicare*. The former means literally to bring into the world, to give birth, and is to be found in such words as the French *éditeur*, the Russian *izdatelstvo* and the German *Verlag* and *herausgeben*. The latter implies the existence of an anonymous mass of prospective readers at the disposal of whom the literary work is put and accounts for such words as the English *publisher*, the French *publier* and the German *Veröffenlichung* or *Verbreitung*.

In the one case attention is directed to the work and its birth, in the other to the unknown reader and his unpredictable reactions.

The mere issuing of a book (in the *edere* sense) is a self-contained and self-justified action, while its publication involves considerable risks. No-one publishing a book can forsee exactly how much attention potential readers will give it. He may make guesses or even forecasts, but he cannot outline in advance the path to be followed by a book which has been put into circulation, he cannot determine the stages and limits of its distribution; in a word, he cannot establish a programme for it. Strictly speaking, publication is non-programmed issuing.

But there is also programmed issuing. The clearest case of this is the sale of a book by advance subscription. As the market is guaranteed by the fact that the volume is paid for in advance, the programming is very strict. It is somewhat less so in the case of book-club editions, but these hem in the potential reader with so many commitments that the dangers of variation may be regarded as reduced to a minimum.

Certain forms of semi-programmed issue bear the same relation to publication in the true sense of the term as ground-bait fishing does to fly fishing. This is the case, for instance, of books distributed within a closed circle whose requirements are known and whose preferences have been thoroughly established. As we have already seen, this applies to most functional books and, more especially, to school-books. But it also applies wherever a specialized public is involved, a group of readers socially distinct from other groups and with readily identifiable characteristics. Devotees of science fiction, for example, or of certain types of detective novels, are often grouped around those somewhat esoteric magazines which Americans call "fanzines". It is easy to establish the tastes of such readers and to foresee their reactions, if only through the letters they write to their favourite magazine. This gives rise to literary production which is both programmed and alive, in that the exchanges which take place around the fanzine keep it from becoming mechanical and cut- and-dried. The same cannot be said, unfortunately, of groups of readers which are too large for communication to be established, but whose tastes are sufficiently similar to be satisfied by rudimentary programming. This applies particularly to a whole section of children's literature which works on a very narrow range of themes and approaches. It applies, above all, to the "photo-novels" or sentimental popular novels which represent a very low level of psychological maturity.

This, incidentally, is the great danger of programmed publication. From the publisher's point of view, it is financially safe; but it impoverishes and sterilizes literary communication precisely because it does away with the element of uncertainty. As far as a large section of literary opinion is concerned, the unforeseeable choice made by the reader is the only way in which he can indicate his aesthetic judgment and cause it to be reflected in production. Non-programmed publication, involving a large number of ventures and relatively few successes, makes a sort of natural selection possible. It may well be felt that natural selection is not the best means of ensuring high quality in literary communication, but it must be recognized that, in the world as it is, it is also one of the few means practicable.

Nor must we minimize the importance of literary works which do not succeed. Success is merely the spectacular aspect of an intellectual and artistic life, which takes many forms. It may be that only one book in a hundred achieves lasting fame; even so, one hundred books have been published and have, all in all, been read by a not insignificant number of readers, one hundred publishing ventures have been carried out by publishers whose selection was made from among hundreds and perhaps thousands of manuscripts submitted by as many potential authors, with all that this implies in the way of intellectual and artistic activity at every level. The intensity and richness of a country's literary life is to be measured not by the number of its best-sellers, but by the number of its writers and readers, by the range of their talents and tastes, by the multiplicity of the exchanges, by the variety of cultural experiments of all kinds. France is neither the largest producer nor the largest consumer of books—far from it—but it is undeniably one of the countries whose literary activity is most intense. Paris is one of the cities where an author receives his laurels, just as a bullfighter receives his in Madrid. Literary books with sales in excess of 10,000 in a given year account for barely 3 or 4% of that year's total production and, at most, for 10% of the strictly literary production; books which fail economically represent—as may easily be calculated—a number of acts of reading at least equal to and probably higher than those in respect of successful books.

This gives us food for thought. Where publishers, avoiding risk, seek to do too much programming and, in particular, are loath to push a book beyond the limits of its original public by means of bold reprintings and energetic sales promotion, they do, of course, keep their firms going, but they forget that their duty and their interest also lie, on the one hand, in giving the unknown writer his chance and, on the other, in ensuring that an established author finds a suitable reward for his work. If other publishers adopt the same attitude, they all run the risk of finding that the intellectual effervescence and restlessness which are the very atmosphere of literary activity have disappeared, and without that effervescence and restlessness books lose their living social support and become consumer goods like any others, like those—as Diderot would say—which are produced in manufactories. They run the risk, in fact, of killing their own jobs.

This being said, the fact remains that too little programming is as bad as too much. Many publishers, especially in Europe, tend to operate on the basis of big hauls, taking in scores or even hundreds of titles. The returns are very low. It is no longer, as Diderot suggested, one book in two which fails but eight or nine in every ten. A publisher who turns out 120 novels a month is not surprised to find that more than a hundred of them are read by only a handful of people.

None the less, he continues on the same lines, thereby proving that, generally (but not invariably), he makes a profit. He does so because the operation is distorted at the outset by the commercial machinery which has grown out of a publishing industry more concerned with security than with expansion. Natural selection, which becomes lethal from the writer's point of view, is largely offset, as far as the publishers are concerned, by the law of large numbers. In this gamble, they win every time or, at any rate, do not lose very much—except, obviously, in the event of persistent ill-luck, inveterate blundering or major shortcomings in organization. Everything is based on experience and on commercial calculation. Experience shows that, given a minimum degree of care in selecting titles, between 4 and 5% of the works published will run to medium-sized printings and one, from time to time, will make its way into the category of very large printings. Commercial calculation reveals that, once a certain sales level has been passed, the scale of profit suddenly changes, so that a single success can offset scores of failures.

A book's retail price is calculated on the cost price of the first printing, which, nine times out of ten, as we have seen, is the only printing. In France, for instance, the maximum retail price, as far as literary works are concerned, is established on the basis of the formula $C = \dfrac{KF}{1-kd}$, C being the retail price, d being the author's royalty per 1 franc of the retail price, k being a coefficient varying according to the rate of such royalties, and F being the unit manufacturing price. In practice this amounts to multiplying the manufacturing price by a coefficient which may vary, depending on the country and the type of book, from 3 to 5. The cheapness of a book depends on the low cost of unit manufacture in the first printing. Since basic printing costs are considerable, the unit manufacturing cost decreases in proportion to the number of copies printed. The whole secret of mass-circulation books is that the initial printing is extremely high, a circumstance which naturally implies tying up considerable capital. Where ordinary non-programmed publication is concerned (and especially literary publication distributed on a limited scale), such risks cannot be afforded, so that, except in the case of an established author, the printing is limited to a number of copies sufficient to provide a reasonable profit at a reasonable retail price. This initial printing generally ranges, depending on the country concerned, from 3,000 to 10,000 copies.

To illustrate these somewhat abstract data, let us take the case—purely theoretical and very much simplified—of a publisher who has paid $5,000 for the type-setting, printing, paper and binding of 5,000 copies of a book (4). The unit cost being $1, he decides to fix the retail price at $5 a copy, the coefficient in this case being 5. We shall assume as a reasonable average that the author's royalties and distribution costs (advertising, commission to salesmen, discount to wholesalers and booksellers, etc.) amount roughly to $66\frac{2}{3}\%$ of the retail price, so that the publisher takes in more or less $1.65 for each copy sold. Before he can make up his accounts, however, he must, no matter what the sale may be, begin by recovering the $5,000 he paid out to the printer and then meet his direct and general overheads (editorial and business salaries, warehousing, shipping, taxes, etc.), which we shall assume for the sake of argument to represent 40% of the investment made in the book concerned—*i.e.*, in this case, $2,000. In order to recover this $7,000, the publisher must sell 4,250 copies of the 5,000 he printed. He reaches then what is known as the "get out" or "break-even" point, and he can expect to make a profit on the sale of the remaining copies, which, by the way, are much less than 750, since two or three hundred have been sent out for review or used for other publicity purposes and a few more given to the author. The yield of those copies will be more or less $700 net—*i.e.*, including the recurring expenses in the investment—a profit of roughly 10%. Should the book sell out within a few months, this rate of interest is not to be lightly dismissed. Where sales are disappointing, the maximum loss amounts to $5,000 or, if recurring expenditure (direct and general overheads) is included, $7,000.

On the other hand, there is no limit to the profits which may be made if the book continues to sell. Let us assume that our publisher reaches the break-even point in six weeks, sees indications that he has a best-seller, and decides to reprint. Let us likewise assume that he is cautious and orders a reprint only of the same size as the original edition. This time he will not pay $5,000 for 5,000 copies since the printer will have kept the type set up. The manufacturing costs of a book are of two kinds. On the one hand, there is what is known as the plant (composition and, eventually, plates), for which the publisher has not to pay again, and on the other hand there is manufacturing proper for which he has to pay in proportion to the size of the printing. The latter includes paper, presswork and binding. Binding is an important item in hard-cover publishing, so that a reprint is always more advantageous in countries like France where even quality books are currently paper-bound. In an article on general publishing in Britain (5) W. G. Taylor states that while producing the printed sheets of a 256-page crown octavo book in a first edition of 3,000 copies costs about £350 (in 1957), a reprint of 1,500 sheets of the same book costs about £120, which means the unit manufacturing price of the reprint (excluding the invariable cost of binding) represents approximately 65% of the original manufacturing price. Of course, the proportion varies according to the size of the original edition.

In our example (a 5,000 copies first printing and a 5,000 copies reprint) we shall admit the unit cost drops by 30%—*i.e.*, from $1 to 70 cents. The retail price, however, does not drop, and the return is still $1.65 per copy sold. The new investment amounts to $3,500 plus $2,000 in recurring costs—*i.e.*, $5,500—from which may be deducted the $500 profit on the first printing, leaving a total of $5,000. As soon as the 3,000th-odd copy of the second printing has been sold, the publisher reaches a new break-even point and, if the second printing sells out, he makes a profit of roughly $3,250, which means that if he wishes to try it again, he needs an additional investment of only $250 for the printer. At this point his profit margin reaches a maximum since, manufacturing costs being practically covered by earlier profits, he has to meet only those running costs which cannot be reduced. This means that if the book has an actual sale of 100,000, he may expect a net profit of well over $50,000.

Before we cry out against this figure, we must remember that a sale of 100,000 is exceedingly rare, at any rate in respect of ordinary editions with a limited distribution. In fact, weighing up chances, a publisher with a single book is hardly any better placed for a comparable gain than the owner of a sweepstake ticket.

Fortunately for the trade there is no such thing as a publisher with a single book. In the long run, failures and successes counterbalance one another, and according to a survey conducted in 1964 by the American Book Publishers Council, only actual sales being taken into account, the average profit represents roughly 9·5% of the manufacturing investment and 4% of the total investment, all overheads included (6).

This is indeed a very narrow margin. It is not surprising, therefore, that publishers should seek methods to avoid risks. One of those methods is a "Malthusian" policy tending to underestimate the prospective sales of a particularly risky book (the first novel of a young writer, for instance) and to satisfy itself with a "cash" breakeven which leaves the care of heavy general overheads to safer ventures. In an article on the management and accounting of the book business (7) George P. Brockway studies the case of an ordinarylength $3.50 novel. Although his methods of calculation are somewhat different from ours, one may easily compare his figures with those we quote above. He first gives the case of a normal edition of 7,500 copies taking the general overhead into account and then that of a "safer" cut-down edition of 5,000 copies which leaves aside the problem of the general overhead. (See table opposite.)

Obviously in the first case the publisher cannot sell 7,759 copies out of a printing of 7,500, while in the second case, if the edition sells out rapidly, he may hope for a *cash* profit of $2,500, which will boost his business and allow him immediate reinvestment in a further venture. In fact, this short-term policy may prove extremely advantageous to him. The trouble is it cannot prove advantageous at all to the author whose gains even in the case of a sell-out will be strictly limited to a bare $1,750. Only a long-range publishing policy—which necessarily takes the general overheads into account and sets the whole operation on a firm financial basis—can give him a fair chance and provide him with an incentive to go on writing.

	Normal edition	Cut-down edition
Investment		
Plant	$1,000	$1,000
Manufacturing	$3,750	$2,750
Advertising	$2,000	$1,500
Total	$6,750	$5,250
Unit sales price	$ 3·50	$ 3·50
Unit costs		
Discounts	1·50	1·50
Royalties	·38	·35
Direct overhead	·10	·10
General overhead	·65	
Total	2·63	1·95
Amount available	·87	1·55
Break-even sale	$\dfrac{\$6,750·00}{\$\ \ ·87}=7,759$	$\dfrac{\$5,250·00}{\$\ \ 1·55}=3,388$

Another method is to rely on the fact that in the long run the publisher's profits are bound to offset his losses, since the latter are limited in extent, while the former are not. Even casting his net at random in the current literary production, a publisher is statistically sure to haul every now and then, among the small fry of unsaleable books, a sufficient percentage of medium- or best-sellers. This is particularly true in a country like France where literary life is both active and varied. Let us assume that a French publisher has completed a publishing programme covering fifteen identical works. Each of these books had a first printing of 3,000 and the total investment, including recurring expenditure and general overhead, amounted to 210,000 francs. Even if only one of these books is reprinted many times and sells 100,000 copies while the others sell none at all (something which never happens), the net profit still amounts to 90,000 francs, a comforting 43% and a very satisfactory return. If we take a more likely eventuality and assume that, out of a programme of one hundred titles, seventy sell an average of 200 copies, ten sell out the first printing, nine sell 20,000 and one sells 100,000, the profit still amounts to some 200,000 francs on an original investment of 1,400,000 francs.

All of this, obviously, is purely theoretical, but it applies in a great many cases. It has very often happened that a single best-seller, published in several hundreds of thousands of copies and intelligently exploited, has kept a publishing house going for several years without being immediately endangered by careless management, errors of judgment and commercial blunders. A great deal of bad publishing can be done under the shelter of a little good publishing. This sort of negative security encourages publishers to avoid making a responsible selection. This is a lottery in which the law of averages always operates in favour of the punter. The result is that the profitability of the venture as a whole is always guaranteed without directly bringing into question the personality of the authors or the quality of their work. It is for this reason that a great part of the literary production (especially fiction) circulating nowadays is made up of slapdash, ill-digested and badly written works which any self-respecting literary editor should either reject out of hand or send back for rewriting.

Hence, non-programmed publishing, like programmed publishing, when carried to excess, leads to economic neutralization of the writer, to a divorce between his profit-earning capacity and that of the publisher. Experience proves that any such divorce invariably results in a deterioration in literary communication. As long as literature was only a socially limited phenomenon, as long as it was possible to regard as literature only those works which are considered by an intellectual *élite* to be good, this deterioration could be overlooked and the works affected by it could be consigned to the underworld of sub-literature. This becomes utterly impossible as soon as literature emerges as an act of mass communication.

Mass-circulation books

The falling hyperbola representing the sales rate of a fast-seller is due to the gradual saturation of the public for which the book was intended. This saturation naturally does not apply to all the individuals making up that public, but only to those to whom this particular book is likely to be of interest—*i.e.*, those who are likely to react consciously and independently on reading it. Doubt as to the identity of the potential readers, together with the impossibility of foreseeing their reactions, is precisely the factor which gives non-programmed publication its creative quality. That a fast-seller should be unable to go beyond a certain distribution is quite natural, since the limits are set by the number of people in the public concerned by that particular book.

This public, moreover, must be sufficiently large to "carry" the book both from an economic and from a literary point of view. In the vast majority of cases, however, this public is a social group which is both narrow and scattered. Even in those countries where the cultural training of the masses has been undertaken on a systematic basis, it is evident that the reading public (which we have already defined as the public capable of independent acts of reading) is not commensurate with the cultivated public (*i.e.*, people capable of making a reasoned judgment of what they read) and, even less, with the real public consisting of the actual book purchasers.

In the large book-producing countries of Western Europe, the real public represents between 3 and 5% of the reading public. The whole machinery for the production and distribution of books is designed with a view to this minority. The ceiling for an ordinary bookshop success can therefore be estimated on the basis of the number making up that public. In France, for example, where the real public numbers approximately one million, the maximum sale for a book distributed through normal bookselling channels may be estimated at roughly 300,000, on the assumption that there is an average of 3·5 acts of reading for each purchaser.

It is very likely that a book reaching this level will already be shaping as a best-seller, since it is inconceivable that all the readers constituting the real public should have been interested in it from the outset. It must first have proved successful with a portion of that public and then, before reaching saturation point, have gone beyond the bounds of this initial group to win over other groups and, step by step, the public at large. Once again it must be pointed out that this crossing of social boundaries constitutes the specific phenomenon of the best-seller. Hence, there may be best-sellers at several levels. The example described above concerns a best-seller within the real public, and, in France, its sales may range from 150,000 to 300,000. Such is the case of a good Prix Goncourt winner. Other best-sellers, even before saturating that portion of the real public which they may reach, begin to gain segments of the literate public which are not ordinarily in the habit of reading. Sales may then be very high indeed, amounting, as far as France is concerned, to between 500,000 and 800,000. In the early years of its existence, Pierre Daninos' *Les Carnets du Major Thompson* was a typical example of this sort of success. It should be noted that the change in the scale of sales does not lead to any significant change either in the distribution or in the presentation of the book. It continues to sell at a high price, in an edition similar to that of books with a limited circulation, and it is purchased mainly in the ordinary bookshops.

The situation is quite different as regards a third type of best-seller which is peculiar to our age. This is the book which goes beyond the limits of the literate public to penetrate the broad masses of the reading public. In this case, other social strata and classes are involved. It is no longer possible to use the same technical processes or to follow the same routes. The book must undergo that mutation which has given rise to the mass-circulation book, the paperback or *livre de poche*. So long as it remained within the bounds of the cultivated public, the book had to do with relatively homogeneous social groups, having comparable social behaviour patterns, living standards, habits, tastes and intellectual background. Beyond those limits, however, it enters unknown territory and everything is changed—price, appearance and selling methods.

One of the reasons why the paperback revolution was so dramatic in the United States is that the real reading public as we defined it earlier never amounted to more than 1 to 2% of the adult literate population. Even now the cultivated readers of regular bookstores are hardly more numerous. This means that the conventional book trade in the United States had to rely on a mass of prospective readers no bigger than the French million and certainly less than half what the British book trade can expect. Indeed, such a situation was clearly reflected in the output figures of the early fifties, when the United States were seventh among book producers, just after France, and halfway from the British Western world leadership. It is also reflected in the distribution of books as it was described in 1958 by Frank L. Schick: "There are about 9,000 outlets of all kinds and sizes for hard-cover books in the United States, of which about half make an effort to handle new, non-specialized books, but only 500 can be considered to be effective stores, adequately stocked; an additional 1,000 stores attempt to offer a fairly good general book service; and 3,000 stores provide at least the most popular modern books." (8)

If we consider that the French network included at that time more than 3,500 regular bookshops—one for each 10,000 adult literate Frenchmen, the American situation certainly looks rather appalling.

The consequences were all the more spectacular when the paperback broke into the mass-circulation network which Frank L. Schick describes as including "nearly 110,000 retail outlets, ranging from newstands on street corners, in subway and railroad stations, bus and air terminals, drug and department stores and supermarkets, to exclusive paperback stores and general and college bookstores". (9)

The mass-circulation book must go where the masses are. It accordingly takes on the appropriate appearance, abandoning the sobriety designed for an *élite* in favour of the vivid colours designed to appeal to mass tastes. And the price, in particular, is brought into line with the prices charged for ordinary consumer goods mass produced by modern industry. When the first Penguin books appeared in 1935, they cost sixpence—*i.e.*, slightly more than 5% of the price of a normal hand-bound volume. Although in the United States 25-cent paperbacks have now disappeared, the average retail price of a mass-circulation paperback is 50 cents—*i.e.*, between 10 and 13% of that of a hard-bound adult trade book. Although the percentage may vary (in France it ranges from 15 to 20%) the price of a mass-circulation book tends in most countries to be no higher than the entrance ticket to a popular cinema. This is true also of socialist countries: in the USSR the price of a paperback novel is roughly 55 kopecks, or about 60 cents.

As we already know, such prices mean huge printings. In the United States, where big business, with its enormous capital and high-power methods, broke into the book trade in the late forties, the initial printing for a mass-circulation paperback is seldom less than 100,000 and is frequently very much higher. In January 1963, for example, Irving Stone's novel *The Agony and the Ecstasy*, which was published by the New American Library in its Signet Series at 95 cents (already a "quality" price), had a first printing of 1,050,000.

It is true that not all printed copies are sold. Unsold paperbacks in the United States represent an estimated 40% of the printings, a much higher proportion than for hard-bound books. On the other hand, the overwhelming invasion of paperback titles is not so clearly reflected in the sales. In the mid-fifties 1,200 paperbacks were published yearly in the United States out of a total book production of 12,000 titles—*i.e.*, a bare 10%—while in the mid-sixties, when the American production reaches close to 30,000 titles a year, paperback titles number nearly 10,000, which means an astounding $33\frac{1}{3}$%. In the same ten years paperback sales climbed only from 250,000,000 copies sold for 50 million dollars to 600,000,000 copies sold for 100 million dollars, which means a comparable proportion of the general volume of the trade.

One of the reasons for this kind of comparative stagnation of sales is the abundance of titles put on the market. The same happened in Britain to Penguin Books, as Sir Allen Lane very clearly explained: "The more choice the reading public is offered, on its limited book-buying budget, the more selective it becomes—with the result that, as the years go by, many titles sell less than their predecessors did. Instead of a first printing of 80,000 or 100,000 copies, therefore, a more prudent current figure will be 40,000 or 50,000 copies—and this cutting-down of printing quantities becomes an element in fixing the selling-price of the book." (10)

Thus a Penguin book which cost 6*d*. when a hard-cover novel was priced 7*s*. 6*d*., now costs 2*s*. 6*d*. when the hard-cover novel is still only 18*s*. In the United States, after the heyday of the 25-cent paperback, prices began a steady climb towards the dollar. At the same time a new type of paperback developed, with a much more conservative financial balance and a much more reduced prospective public. Those "quality" paperbacks, sold for 95 cents to 2 dollars and more, cannot be considered as a mere reinvention of the French *livre broché*. They differ from the mass paperback only by the fact that they aim at a limited public which is still "a mass", but not *any* mass, which of course reduces the risks.

A very significant feature of the quality paperback trade is that it much more readily publishes new books than the mass paperback: 75% of the latter are reprints, while 57% of the former are new books. In fact, the quality paperback is an attempt—the future will say if it is a successful attempt—to cope with the problem of programming in mass publishing.

Low prices demand huge printings, but huge printings demand enormous investments. A hard-bound novel can be published in the conventional way for a few thousand dollars, while a paperback publisher may have to pay several hundred thousand dollars in royalties, printing, advertising, before he is likely to receive a cent. It will be appreciated that a non-programmed edition can hardly be considered for this type of book. The cumulative risk would be too great, and it would be impossible to find sufficient capital to ensure that the law of large numbers came into play.

The American literary paperback is therefore most often a reissue of a book which has already proved itself or is in process of proving itself a best-seller among the literate public. This is the only way of reducing the hazards. The same does not apply to the functional paperback, the very nature of which makes strict programming possible since it is designed to meet an identifiable need. Although it may seem paradoxical, scientific books are the ones which can most readily be adapted to the requirements of mass distribution. It was a scientific collection, the *Que sais-je?* series, which first used the formula successfully in France. By systematically introducing the paperback into universities, the Americans have managed to make libraries less like museums, turning them into consumption centres where students find themselves in the very heart of the living world of books and can engage in daily intercourse with those books (11).

As far as literary books are concerned, it is infinitely harder to establish intercourse with the consumer. The mass-circulation book as it is at present conceived, and as it is conditioned by our social structures—more especially, the social structures of the Western world—provides the masses, in what may be called a dictatorial way, with works called forth by and designed for narrower social groups. Here we find ourselves, at the level of social strata and classes, confronted with the same problem of "bestowed" or "imposed" literature which, at the national level, we found between literary high-pressure and low-pressure zones.

If, for example, we consider French production of the pocketbook type, we see that, in the literary sector at any rate, most publishers have restricted themselves to two types of books: as regards contemporary literature, to best-sellers of all kinds; as regards earlier literature, to works considered of importance in literary history as seen by the universities. At first glance, this might seem to furnish adequate material, and, in the enthusiasm aroused by novelty, the reader is amazed at coming on cheap editions of texts which have become unfindable or inaccessible. In this latter respect, he is quite right, but this apparent abundance is misleading. Year in, year out, a country like France publishes between 150 and 200 successful books, of which barely twenty are genuine best-sellers. As for the classics, the stock of those remaining to be rediscovered is by no means inexhaustible. The thousand or so authors who make up the historical image of French literature as seen by scholars (and the list includes the lesser known authors) have at most produced 5,000 or 6,000 works which are really suitable for mass distribution or, indeed, for distribution of any kind. Even if translations be added, this gives a corpus of only a few thousand older titles, to which are added, at best, two or three hundred modern titles a year, and nothing further can be expected from programmed literary publication which is restricted to certainties, and will not run the risks inherent in trial and error. This is quite inadequate to sustain a publishing trade and, above all, to arouse and maintain genuine intellectual activity among the masses.

Penguin Books in Great Britain recognized the problem long ago and have attempted to solve it, but the solutions so far tried have been no more than palliatives. If we look closely at the Penguin output, we find that the firm is kept going by the programmed sector, whether in the form of the functional books of the Pelican series, the children's Puffin books, the green-covered mystery and crime thrillers, or reprints of standard works in the main Penguin series. Compared with this huge programmed production, the attempts made to branch out into new fields seem insignificant, even if some of them—such as the famous experimental Penguin New Writing— have had a beneficial influence on British literary life. It is, besides, doubtful whether, at any rate until recently, the Penguin management really thought in terms of real mass publication. Even now, as we have seen, they feel that their books are designed for an *élite*.

The fact is that they derive originally from an *élite*, and this is the great difficulty. Various efforts have been made in France and Germany over recent years to inject new blood into mass-circulation books, but such efforts have always come from fairly narrowly delimited cultivated circles, and often, indeed, from literary cliques. We have left the socialist countries out of account, since their publishing is always more or less programmed and their books are always, in principle, aimed at the masses.

The problem of the mass-circulation book therefore remains untouched. By making works produced by the cultivated sector available to a far greater readership than they have ever had before, publishers may save literary life from the emptiness, sterility and decline to which undue concentration on non-programmed publication in the erroneous fashion outlined above may reduce it; but such books are still none the less "imposed" books, eliciting no response. It is a fact that literary criticism does not give the same place to mass editions as to traditional editions, even in the United States, where publishers command enormous means of propaganda (12). In France, it was ten years before the main literary papers paid any attention to pocket books (13).

And even if the literary critics and literary periodicals were to give particular attention to such books, the problem would not be solved, since the literary opinion reflected in such criticism and such periodicals is still that of the cultivated public. We shall always discover without difficulty how an intellectual or a semi-intellectual reacts to a popular success which has run its course in a few weeks, but we shall not know the reactions of the office worker, the factory hand or the housewife who has suddenly come upon Sartre, Goethe or Homer through a chance purchase in the local chain store.

NOTES

(1) Denis Diderot, *Lettre historique et politique adressée à un magistrat sur le commerce de la librairie*, June 1767, pp. 38–39.

(2) For concrete case studies, see Jean Hassenforder, *Etude de la diffusion d'un succés de librairie*, multigraphed document from the Centre d'Etudes Economiques, Paris, 1957. See also Dr Peter Meyer-Dohm, *Der Westdeutsche Büchermarkt*, *op. cit.*, *passim*.

(3) Hans Ferdinand Schulz, *Das Schicksal der Bücher und der Buchhandel*, 2nd edition, Berlin, 1960.

(4) See Daniel Melcher, *Trade Book Marketing in the United States*, in *Book Distribution and Promotion in South Asia*, edited by N. Sankaranarayanan, Unesco and Higginbothams, Madras, no date, pp. 140–8.

(5) W. G. Taylor, *General Publishing* (p. 50), in *The Book World Today*, edited by John Hampden, London, Allen and Unwin, 1957.

(6) This figure is drawn from the very interesting study *L'industrie et le commerce du livre aux Etats-Unis*, published by J. Mame, President of the Centre de Productivité du Livre, in *Bibliographie de la France*, Nos. 21–22, 25 May and 1 June 1965.

(7) George P. Brockway, *Business, Management and Accounting* (pp. 226–228), in *What Happens in Book Publishing*, edited by Chandler B. Grannis, New York, Columbia U.P., 1957. See also *Break-even Point on Novels: What Cost Factors are Involved*, in *Publishers' Weekly*, 12 October 1964, p. 27.

(8) Frank L. Schick, *The Paperbound Book in America*, Bowker, New York, 1958, p. 102.

(9) *Ibid.*, p. 103.

(10) Sir Allen Lane, *Paper-bound books* (p. 104), in *The Book World Today*, *op. cit.*

(11) See *Paperbacks in the Schools*, New York, Bantam Books, 1963.

(12) See Jay Tower, *Reviewing Paperbounds*, in *Publishers' Weekly*, 11 September 1961, pp. 30–33.

(13) See the special numbers of *Lettres Françaises*, No. 1051, 29 October–4 November 1964, and of *Les Temps Modernes*, Nos. CCXXVII and CCXXVIII, April and May 1965.

Bookshops and Mass Circulation

The cultivated circuit and the popular circuit

CAN books become not only a medium of mass communication but also the basis for a mass literature solely through sales in chain stores and drugstores? The answer to this is contained in a second question: are chain stores and drugstores equipped to create that communication between the producer of books and the consumer of books which we now know to be indispensable to any literary activity?

The special feature of the traditional bookshop is that it is, or should be, organized with such communication in mind, which is not the case with the book counter of a store or even with a news-stand selling books as a sideline. The ideal solution would therefore seem to be to channel all books through the bookshops. Unfortunately, these shops are instruments for limited distribution and are, for the most part, accessible to the cultivated section of the population only. Naturally there is no law or regulation which imposes this social limitation, but it is just as much imposed by opening hours and geographical location. In an article published in 1957, Bénigno Cacérès observed that, "With few exceptions, bookshops selling serious novels are not to be found on the routes used by the ordinary worker." (1) This means that in the course of his everyday movements, the worker has virtually no occasion to pass by a bookshop when it is open for business, and, when the opportunity does occur, he has no sufficient motive to inspire him to go in and buy a book.

This situation was highlighted by the survey conducted in Bordeaux in 1960–61 concerning the distribution of book sales-points in the city (2). There is much evidence that the observations made during that survey are applicable to most cities in Western Europe and the United States.

A distinction was drawn in this survey between *bookshops*, whether large or small, which sell books mainly and have an independent business policy, and *bookstalls* or *sales-points* which are distribution units without real responsibility, book sales dominating in some and being of secondary importance in others.

The bookshop as distinct from the bookstall or sales-point is therefore distinguished by the extent to which the bookseller is aware of his public. The extent of this awareness can be very easily measured: one need only compare the window display with the stock available for sale inside the shop. The window is the face which the bookshop shows the world and hence reflects the image of itself and its activity which the bookseller would like to convey to his fellow citizens and potential clients. It reflects, in short, the image of a theoretical, ideal reader. On the other hand, the stocks inside represent the experimentally established reality of the actual public which frequents the shop.

The difference between the window contents and the shop contents therefore indicates how far the actual customers differ from the customers desired, and this discrepancy itself demonstrates how far the bookseller is commercially independent. If his attitude is passive, if he carries on his trade mechanically, there is no reason why there should not be absolute identity between the contents of the window and the contents inside. If, on the other hand, he is trying to find the part he should play, to place himself in relation to the public, then significant differences may be expected to emerge.

And, in fact, they do emerge. Diagram 3 gives a comparative analysis of Bordeaux bookshops and bookshop windows. The figures shown as ordinates are the percentages of businesses of the various types offering books of the kind shown as abscissae either in their windows (thin line) or in the shops themselves (thick line).

One point is immediately apparent: the contents of the window and of the shop itself coincide exactly in the case of bookstalls and more or less exactly in that of sales-points: there is no discrepancy between the commercial reality and the social image. On the other hand, there is a very definite discrepancy in the bookshops and, more especially, in the large bookshops, which generally have a complete range of all types of books but systematically keep out of their windows—besides second-hand books, which are a special branch of the trade—popular novels, thrillers, mass paperbacks and, for the opposite reason, more serious literature, the latter no doubt

DIAGRAM 3
Window Contents and Shop contents

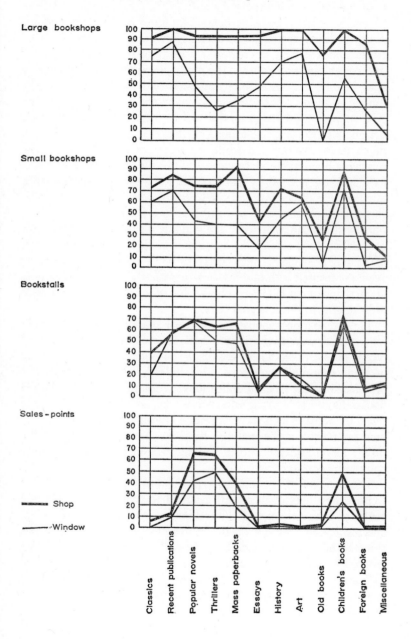

Large bookshops

Small bookshops

Bookstalls

Sales - points

━━━━━ Shop

━━━━━ Window

Classics
Recent publications
Popular novels
Thrillers
Mass paperbacks
Essays
History
Art
Old books
Children's books
Foreign books
Miscellaneous

being regarded as too dull even for the ordinary cultivated customer.

Bookshops, therefore, are the only establishments which are deliberately aimed at a clearly defined group of customers and which recognize their customers as such. They are accordingly the only establishments likely to create the conditions required for a sort of intercommunication between the producers and the consumers. But it is obvious that this intercommunication must remain strictly limited. The exclusions and omissions in the booksellers' windows give sufficient indication of the social groups for which they are designed. In the large bookshops, the fact that thrillers are kept very much in the background while more serious literature is given a relatively honourable place calls to mind the stereotyped attitudes (which do not necessarily reflect actual patterns of behaviour) of the intellectual middle class and the liberal professions. In the smaller shops, thrillers move up and more serious literature comes down, but the discrepancy between the window display and the contents of the shop itself is none the less considerable in respect of all types of "popular" books. It may therefore be thought that we are once again confronted with middle-class readers whose cultural attitudes are perhaps somewhat less exclusive, but who are still very conscious of belonging to the educated class.

The fact that bookshops as a whole are specially designed to cater for the small cultivated public is demonstrated by their treatment of recent publications. These are displayed both in the windows and inside in almost all bookshops. This, indeed, is a distinctive feature of bookshops, for recent publications are found only in 60% of the bookstalls and 10% of the sales-points. But such publications, in the sense of books which have appeared during the previous twelve months, represent the material from which the cultivated reader makes his considered choice and by reference to which literary opinion takes shape.

The location of the various types of businesses reveals similar trends. The bookshops are all grouped together in the shopping centre or in the vicinity of cultural institutions such as schools and universities, but are not on the routes normally taken by workers going to or returning from their jobs. The meeting points (more especially, bus stops) around which they mostly have occasion to walk are situated in residential areas on the outskirts of the town or in industrial areas where there are virtually no bookshops. Even those who work in the business areas seldom have occasion to use the streets in which the bookshops are situated, at any rate when these are open.

On the other hand, the sales-points and bookstalls are widely scattered. There are several in practically every district. While means of transport did not appear to affect the cultivated circuit, they play a most important part in this latter case. There are bookstalls in all stations and very often a sales-point near the main bus stops. It is particularly noteworthy that in those areas where workers leave their buses or trains and, more especially, in a sort of ring around the shopping centre, there is a marked concentration of tobacconists where books are sold.

Allowing for the variations due to different social structures and cultural levels from country to country, the same pattern recurs everywhere: a double distribution system comprising two circuits, one having all the resources and habits required for literary intercourse but catering only for a limited section of the population, and the other aimed at the population as a whole but able to serve for communication in one direction only.

It is therefore obvious that no genuine mass literature can emerge and develop unless responsible booksellers conscious of the part they have to play agree to change their approach sufficiently to serve the huge public of the ordinary man and woman who have hitherto been left to what might be called an "authoritarian" distribution machinery. This implies a complete recasting of bookshop structures, a re-evaluation of the nature of the book trade and a revision of its obligations. But if this is to be possible, bookshops must not be misunderstood by the society they are called upon to serve.

The traditional image of bookshops

From the statistician's standpoint, the book trade is lumped together with furniture, boots and shoes, hardware and textiles under the general heading of non-food trades. Booksellers are looked on as book merchants—*i.e.*, as retailers handling objects manufactured from a raw material, which happens to be paper, and processed by certain techniques, which happen to be those of the printing trade. From a strictly economic angle, it must be admitted that this definition of the bookseller is as good as any other (3).

The authorities have not always displayed the same detachment as the economists in regard to bookshops. Books are not only objects made out of paper, but also a medium for communicating thought.

The bookseller who distributes them is in an exposed position at the end of the chain of communication which spreads information and culture throughout a country. It is a position which inevitably attracts official attention, disturbs the authorities and arouses in them a desire to control the distribution of commodities as dangerous and as effective as books. Ever since bookshops came into existence, all authoritarian régimes have done their best to shackle them with strict rules and regulations.

It may reasonably be argued, therefore, that the authorities are aware of the phenomenon of the book trade only so far as it forms part of a group activity which they consider important: the retail trade for the dissemination cf information and culture. These are unquestionably group activities covering the book trade, but to regard bookshops only in terms of such activities is to disfigure them, distort them and rob them of their very nature. They are no longer seen whole and round, as a specific phenomenon. Their position in community life suffers both quantitatively and qualitatively.

The quantitative distortion is perhaps the most obvious and dramatic. Bookshops represent a major element in the life of the community, as may be seen from such elementary considerations as the space occupied by their displays in the streets of a town or the time spent by a given social category in reading books purchased from bookshops; but, if we consider them in terms of retail trade, we are forced to recognize that they are not among the most important branches. Their turnover cannot be compared with that of the food trade or even that of sanitary engineering or household electrical appliances. Furthermore, if we consider them as a part of the communications machinery, we are obliged to admit that as a mass medium they cannot compete with the cinema, with radio or with television, even though mass distribution has, of recent years, given books a greater measure of influence.

Qualitatively, the situation is still worse. Even when States recognize the existence of the cultural phenomenon, provide an administrative structure for it, a budget and perhaps even a Minister, booksellers are looked on as "tainted" because of their commercial or technical interests and are treated like the money-changers in the temple, if not indeed worse. Education and religion are protected by a variety of powerful taboos, yet, in certain respects, are also mass-communication phenomena, indeed economic phenomena, and have been studied as such by sociologists. But culture and especially literature are still realms where, as far as many countries are concerned, the awe of the sacred overrides social perspicacity (4). Yet it is obvious that, were there no bookshops, there might be writers but they would very often go hungry. When we consider the decisive influence which the need to live has had on the emergence or orientation of a given basic literary work, we cannot but be struck by the essential nature of the economic relationship between writer and bookseller.

Whether they will or not, then, booksellers are regarded by their countries' authorities as dealers in printed paper on the same basis as newspaper vendors. Booksellers, moreover, often do sell newspapers as well. Whatever view may be taken of it, the sale of newspapers often provides a very useful support, as far as the public is concerned, for the sale of books. "Pure" bookshops are rare and, of all the supplementary activities which accompany bookselling, the sale of newspapers is far and away the commonest (5). In the socialist countries where an effort is made to apply a policy to the book trade, it is effective only so long as books are not separated from newspapers at distribution level. This situation offers great advantages but also considerable disadvantages, including the fact that the public is often inclined as a result to confuse two activities which, while they may be complementary, are none the less very different one from the other.

The public's notion of the nature of bookshops, moreover, is very vague, even vaguer than that of governments, since the latter are at least compelled to establish their policy in terms of clear and distinct categories, even if these are not always in line with reality. This does not apply to consumers, who regard consumer products, and hence those who distribute them, in terms of a need to be satisfied rather than in terms of a community activity. Whether produced locally or imported, whether paid for in francs, dollars or pounds, coal is always a fuel and the coal merchant is the man who ensures that the kitchen stove or the heating system keeps on working. As far as the housewife is concerned, the only difference between the coal merchant and the supplier of fuel oil, electricity, gas or any other means of producing heat lies in the varying cost or degree of convenience. Problems of national or international power policy are on quite a different level, more especially as domestic consumption of fuels has only a slight bearing on them. Exactly the same situation prevails as regards the attitude of the public towards booksellers. Booksellers are people who supply reading matter. Since newspapers represent an enormous proportion of reading matter, booksellers are basically no different from newspaper vendors.

In discussing bookshops, therefore, we are confronted with a fluid and variable concept which encompasses disparate phenomena with no points of comparison between them. To this must be added what might be called the archaeological strata of the word, since there is no word which does not have a certain semantic memory attached to it and, in the case of words relating to literature, this is particularly pronounced. We must not forget that booksellers existed before printing, and that it is only a relatively short time since the emergence of the publisher deprived them of most of their responsibilities and left them with only the least spectacular, which, however, is also the most formidable, of these responsibilities.

As may be seen, then, the position of the bookseller is by no means clear cut. We can now appreciate some of the reasons for the indefiniteness which hinders the practice of the trade and is disastrous as far as the organization of the profession is concerned. In the eyes of the authorities and of the general public, alike, booksellers are always defined by reference to problems which are not specifically theirs and in which they represent only one element, and by no means the most important. Dealer in printed paper, distributor of information and culture, supplier of reading matter—all these descriptions undoubtedly apply to booksellers, but cannot possibly by themselves suffice to define their functions.

This is perhaps because no effort has ever been made to define them on the basis of books as such, and this omission, in turn, is perhaps due to the fact that we do not know exactly what a book is, even supposing a book to be always the same thing. The only useful definition of a book is one which takes account of the use made of it and is based on literary or functional communication as described at the beginning of this study.

We can then appreciate how far the definition of booksellers in terms of book sales falls short of perfection. Booksellers sell books because someone has to recover the costs of manufacture and distribution and, at the same time, pay for the services rendered, but it is not hard to imagine systems whereby books would be given away for nothing without booksellers ceasing to be what they actually are —one of the channels whereby literary opinion influences production, one of the aspects of literary production offered to literary opinion.

Bookshops and social environment

It must, however, be admitted that, technically speaking, bookshops come under the heading of retail trade. As such—but only as such—they are subject to the economic laws governing trade. Books are something more than packaged goods, and the distribution of reading material is something more than the mere provision of a service (6). In his *Lettre sur la Librairie* from which we have already quoted, where Diderot pointed out that other unsold merchandise still retains some value whereas unsold books have none, he also made the following observation which is no less clear-sighted: "Books are not the same as machines whose effect can be shown by testing, they are not the same as inventions which can be checked in a hundred different ways, they are not the same as secrets whose success has been demonstrated. The success even of a good book depends on an infinite number of circumstances, rational or unpredictable, which not all the shrewdness of self-interest can foresee." (7)

This passage sums up the two problems peculiar to the book trade which make it different from any other trade—the problem of selection and the problem of stocking. How is the bookseller to tell what, in an enormous output, will prove saleable, before the full weight of unsold items affects the balance of his business, and how is he, at the same time, to hold a stock large enough to enable the public to choose freely? He may seek to escape from this dilemma by becoming the passive sales representative of large publishing houses or distribution networks, but he is then no longer a bookseller. He may take refuge in the sale of safe items to a restricted circle of customers, but he thereby cuts himself off from all that is vital in his trade and dooms himself to mediocrity and stagnation. On the other hand, he may protect his business from the danger of idle stock by speculating on the latest publications, but this is a dangerous game in that it implies a constantly changing clientèle: readers remain faithful to their own discoveries and failure to follow up a book, an author or a type of literature means dismissing the public responsible for their success.

This brings us back to the fact that books are undefinable. The story is told of a certain country with a great many generals where it was decided to present a rare and valuable edition of an old book to a general about to retire. The old soldier looked at the volume and remarked, "A book? What's the point? I've already got one!"

The anecdote provides an amusing illustration of the specific difference between books and other consumer goods, between the provision of reading matter and other services. When butchers sell meat, when garage owners repair cars, when chemists recommend a particular soap, their activities are of interest to all those who eat, travel and wash—*i.e.*, virtually all their fellows. When a bookseller sells a book, what he does is of interest only to those to whom that book means something. With certain differences in convenience or enjoyment, one piece of meat can be substituted for another, and the same applies to cars and soaps. But a given book cannot be replaced by another, each act of reading is a particular, individual adventure which cannot be reproduced, replaced or imitated.

It therefore follows that the placing of a book on sale is not comparable with the same operation for any other product. It excludes advertising of the usual kind. Anyone wanting to sell soap puts up posters in the street, since theoretically he is appealing to everybody. The efficiency of his advertising must be calculated in terms of the total number of those who notice it. On the other hand, any given book appeals only to a group which is, simultaneously, determinate as regards its tastes and indeterminate as regards its make-up, social level and geographical distribution. The use of the hoardings in these circumstances would necessarily give only an insignificant return in comparison with the cost involved, since it has to be calculated, not on the total number of those who notice the advertisements, but on the unidentifiable fraction who may be interested by the book.

The programming of publishing obviously makes it possible to isolate large groups of specialized readers and justifies a certain type of group-directed advertising but, if the same system were to be extended to all publishing, it would mean abandoning any selection, that vital selection which, as we have seen, may be the fundamental hazard of publishing but also ensures its vitality and creative power. Advertising in the book trade cannot be other than selective and aimed at a clearly defined public. This means, in a word, that programming, while dangerous at the publishing level, is essential at the bookshop level. It is for this reason, incidentally, that book-clubs, door-to-door bookselling and sales by direct mail all represent serious competition with the traditional type of bookshop. These various methods of selling consist, in fact, in approaching customers who have been singled out and identified and who, in any case, are not anonymous. In the United States those marginal types of bookselling have developed in proportion to the inadequacy of the regular bookshop network. This leads American publishers to enormous distribution expenses, to an inordinate amount of advertising which represents often more than 10% of the total volume of trade. The system is disastrously inefficient for the publishers are not aware of their real or prospective customers, and no programming of retail distribution is possible.

Of all those involved in the book trade, only the bookseller is in direct contact with the reader. He is, so to speak, the sensitive antenna of the structure. Like a front-line soldier who simultaneously carries out the orders of his commanding officers and keeps those officers informed about the terrain, the enemy, his own requirements and the progress of the battle, thereby contributing to the preparation of later orders to be carried out, so the bookseller, while acting as an agent for the literary producer, must also act as his guide and adviser. His stock of recent publications constitutes the testing-ground which should enable him, if not to bring into focus the fact that literature is not necessarily a matter of history—a long-term task which belongs to criticism—at any rate to determine what is viable in literary production and to act appropriately.

The two main concerns which should govern the bookseller's policy and, more especially, its adaptation to the environment, are to detect from the reactions of the first readers the image of what is likely to survive and then to find among the general public those other readers—the "steady readers", so to speak, following the pioneers—who are awaiting this production and will give it their support.

A bookshop must be organized and managed differently depending on whether it is situated in a large city and aimed at the passing trade, whether it is an all-purpose bookshop in a village, or a utility bookshop in a housing complex, but, in all cases, the bookseller must adjust to the threefold necessity of seeking potential readers in the surrounding population, of being situated on routes taken by the population in the course of their daily activities, and of awakening that response which alone enables literary intercommunication to develop.

It will no longer be possible for the booksellers of the future to remain in their shops and wait for customers to turn up. Like it or not, they will have to become some of the cultural leaders in the place where they live, whether it be village, district of a town or housing complex. This is a task which is already beyond the scope of individual resources, and booksellers are entitled to expect the collective power of the publishing industry to provide them with the necessary support and opportunities, while they are likewise entitled to demand of the public conscience that books should have the benefit of the same infrastructures as other mass-communication media and artistic techniques—cinema, radio and television. As Joffre Dumazedier, the sociologist of leisure, has written, "Book distribution must become a process of permanent conquest, as otherwise the forces hostile to reading are likely to gain the victory because of their powerful publicity resources. Publishers and booksellers must apply to books some of the mass-information techniques used by film producers and distributors." (8) We might go even further and urge that publishers and booksellers must themselves invent new publicity and sales techniques. Door-to-door selling, vending-machines, participation surveys, reading clubs and many other methods, if handled by a professional and responsible bookseller, offer a whole range of possibilities from which a choice can be made according to the demands of the environment and the distributor's intentions.

It must be repeated that conscious demands and conscious intentions are both needed. The distribution of reading matter—distribution and consumption—is not an operation allowing of neutrality. It is a militant activity which must always be based on a certain ideology, even if it is only a cultural ideology that is involved. We need only remember that the advance of Methodism in England, rationalist teaching in France and Marxist propaganda in the USSR lay at the roots of some of the most outstanding successes in the realm of books considered as a source of culture.

Booksellers must therefore regard themselves as the agents of continuing cultural activity, whose connection with books does not end with the selling of them. In this, they resemble those other distributors of reading matter, the librarians. Little has been said in this study about libraries, because their position is still not fully understood. In most countries, libraries are only just beginning to emerge from the tradition which regarded them as places for the preservation rather than the consumption of books.

The latest statistics none the less indicate that reading in public libraries is particularly flourishing in those countries which are also major consumers of books from bookshops. This makes it clear that the two methods of distribution, far from being competitive, complement each other. They are subject to the same constraints and the same demands. It would be as illusory to set up public libraries in a country or social environment which lacked the cultural channels needed for literary communication as it would be to open bookshops there for the sale of books created in another world. Libraries and bookshops can, however, co-operate in order to create the conditions needed for cultural communication.

Reading at the place of employment represents one of the areas most favourable to co-operation of this type (9). We are beginning to appreciate the vital importance of factory libraries in the cultural awakening of the workers. Factory libraries are socially effective only if their establishment and management spring from interest shown by the workers themselves, but they are culturally worth while only if they operate in liaison with booksellers and educationists, without thereby being subjected to commercial pressure from the former or didactic pressure from the latter.

The balance is not easy to maintain, but books, after all, are "reading machines", and what applies to other machines is also true of them. Between the liberation they offer and the subjection they may impose, the slightest touch is enough to alter the balance.

NOTES

(1) Bénigno Cacérès, *Comment conduire le livre au lecteur?* in *Informations Sociales*, Paris, January 1957, No. 1, p. 107.

(2) Concerning the subsequent discussion and Diagram 3, see Robert Escarpit and Nicole Robine, *Atlas de la Lecture à Bordeaux*, Centre de Sociologie des Faits Littéraires, Faculté des Lettres et Sciences Humaines, Bordeaux, 1963.

(3) The substance of this chapter was elaborated by the author in a paper presented at the 2nd International Booksellers' Congress, Paris, Unesco, 1964, under the title *Le Libraire, le pouvoir et le public*.

(4) In this connection, see Gilbert Mury's article, *Une sociologie du livre est-elle possible?* in *Informations Sociales*, Paris, January 1957, No. 1, pp. 64–70.

(5) Only three 'pure' bookshops were found in Bordeaux out of fifty-two. On the other hand, 12% of the large bookshops sold newspapers as a secondary activity, and 28% of the small bookshops as a main or secondary activity. 60% of the bookstalls also sold newspapers.

(6) The author expanded the substance of this section in a paper presented at the XXXth Congrès National des Libraires de France, Paris, Unesco, 1964, under the title *L'adaptation de la librairie au milieu.*

(7) *Op. cit.,* p. 15.

(8) J. Dumazedier, *Vers une civilisation du loisir?,* Paris, 1962, pp. 175–203.

(9) A participation survey has been under way since 1962 at the Centre de Sociologie des Faits littéraires de Bordeaux, initially under the direction of J. Boussinesq and latterly under that of H. Marquier. See J. Boussinesq, *La lecture dans les bibliothèques d'entreprise de l'agglomération bordelaise,* Centre de Sociologie des Faits littéraires, Faculté des Lettres et Sciences humaines, Bordeaux, 1963. Another instalment is being prepared under the direction of H. Marquier. A symposium on libraries in places of employment was also organized in November 1961 at Unesco by the French National Commission for Unesco, which published a report on the proceedings.

3

Towards a New Form of Communication

The writer's position

THE writer has not yet found his place in the contemporary community. The reason for this is perhaps that the modern community is an enormous mutual-security structure designed to protect its members from the hazards of nature in the raw and man's estate. But there is no way of protecting writers as such. True, they can be given the same social security as all other citizens, old-age pensions, free medical care, and legal aid, but they cannot be insured against their literary hazards.

We are now sufficiently well acquainted with the mechanics of literary life to appreciate that the writer proposes and the public disposes—and so it must be. Literature is born out of this intercommunication, derives its sustenance therefrom and develops because of it. But it is a murderous system in the sense that, for every thousand works conceived, ten come to birth and one to maturity. The proportion can, of course, be improved by various technical devices, notably by broadening the social bases of intercommunication, by improving distribution channels, by giving the reader better and more frequent opportunities of expressing his considered judgment, but the hazards cannot be eliminated nor even reduced to any significant extent. All efforts at really effective programming end up by fixing literature in a rut when they are applied to the filter of publishing. When applied to the writer, they lead purely and simply to sterility.

It is for this reason that success is a form of literary death. A writer's success is not quite the same as a publisher's. It is not enough for a book to sell well and provide a certain return. How indeed could we calculate the interest on an investment reckoned in terms of life, thought and action? Whatever his financial gains, the writer never recovers his capital; he works without security. We can, none the less, accept an economic definition of a writer's success: it is the point at which the sales of one of his books enable him to live by his writing. This point, moreover, represents another aspect of success —the point at which a writer saturates his possible public. However we may look at the matter, it is from this point onwards that the writer is regarded as such by a certain social group which will never again release him, which will never again leave him his freedom, which will impose on him a particular image of himself and which, with the very understandable and natural complicity of the publisher, will, so to speak, "programme" him arbitrarily.

"Never go back the way you came," said Kipling, speaking of literary success. Unless the writer has sufficient strength to tear himself away from his success, to hold himself aloof from it, and even— as has been done—to embark on his career afresh under another name, he is inevitably doomed within ten or fifteen years at most— by which time his original public will have grown older—at best to sterility and at worst to oblivion.

Nothing therefore can save the writer from the necessity of running risks and of doing so alone. Even so, the cards should not be stacked against him, as they may be—and generally are—in two different ways—economically and psychologically.

We have already referred to the disastrous discrepancy between the publisher's profit and that of the writer. There is nothing new in this, and the starving poet is a familiar literary figure. Even in the days when an enlightened prince might act as patron to some man of letters, it was at best a subsistence allowance which he provided. Louis XIV's privy purse supplied the King's protégés with no more than the income of a journeyman printer. In the twentieth century, it can readily be calculated that, to enjoy the standard of living of a skilled linotype operator, a novelist would have to produce a book every eighteen months which sold between 8,000 and 10,000 copies—which is most unusual and indeed extremely improbable (1).

There are numerous alternative solutions to enable writers to survive: a second profession, literary "fringe" activities, journalism, translation, criticism, the economic support of other and more profitable media such as radio, television, films, etc. All these solutions have the drawback that they are not really solutions but merely loopholes, evading the real problem—that of giving the writer back a place in the commercial circuit of the book trade, and linking the return on creative activity to that of publishing activity (2).

The problem, moreover, is infinitely more complex than in the days of Louis XIV or even Diderot. Our society demands something more than the mere survival of its citizens. The writer must not only be given an opportunity to live by his writing, he must also be assured of a standard of living appropriate to the needs of his profession. The myth of the romantic poet who can prove his genius only by dying of cold and hunger in a garret is a deliberate falsehood spread by emergent capitalism with a view to dissociating brain workers from men of action and keeping the intellectual at a distance from economic and social concerns.

Modern thinking demands that the writer's profession be organized within the community, but other problems thereupon arise. The myth of the intellectual worker cherished by emerging socialist societies is no less dangerous than that of the starving poet. It is an appealing phrase which expresses an abstract economic relationship but does not necessarily represent any real, living integration of the writer into the working world. Whether we like it or not, and no matter what the structure of society, literary creation implies a certain freedom to command one's time which—at any rate in the present state of technology—is incompatible with the constraints imposed on the manual worker, either in industry or on the land. Physical or nervous fatigue is not literary. It is probably more difficult to be a worker-writer than a worker-priest. The proletarian writer must choose between solitude among his own kind and social exile. If he chooses exile, even as a State artist, even as a paid member of a writers' union, even as an employee of a publishing firm, he may well find himself isolated or treated as an inferior within another way of life, and may forget the overwhelming reality of the things he stands for, retaining only a bitter, negative philosophy. He may even —and this is something very serious—pass over the pleasures of the common people because he feels them to be degrading. Only a very great artist and a very great man can understand and make others understand that such terms as "popular" and "vulgar" do not necessarily imply inferiority.

Criticism and literary opinion

In a book full of feeling and good sense, the French critic André Thérive raises the problem of the attitude of critics towards what he calls infra-literature, or what others term sub-literature or marginal literature. He does so as a cultivated man subscribing to traditional values, but with a striking clearsightedness. Though he does not accept a sociological conception of literature, he brings out perfectly the social imbalance which affects its future: "As education spreads, and with it the ability to read, an enormous public of readers is spreading out around the small cultivated public." (3) In particular, he recognizes the paradox inherent in the fact that the cure may be worse than the disease and that the solution of the problem raises still more serious problems: "Literature will never be reconciled with society so long as society is at variance with itself, in other words, without common principles and natural hierarchies. And when order is restored, people will undoubtedly regret the present easy-going anarchy under which literature is merely a game played by fewer people and less respected than basketball." (4) At once despairing and apprehensive of the eventual establishment of such a society without cultural classes, André Thérive, for his part, prefers that form of freedom represented by the dilettantism of the expert amateur: "Literary criticism is not a court of law but a picturesque and essential stall on the fairground, somewhere between the lucky dip, the menagerie, the sweetmeat stall and the 'chamber of horrors'." (5)

Appearances notwithstanding, André Thérive here comes very close to providing a human and viable solution to the difficult problem inherent in establishing values for mass-circulation literature. He rejects the authoritarian, standard-setting criticism, with its stiff-necked didactic approach, which lays down the law from outside without regard to the realities of life, but he also rejects the absence of criticism, the commercial neutralism, the statistical indifference of chain-store sales. His picturesque little fairground stall has the merit of rejecting neither the proximity of the humble, everyday pleasures of the crowd nor the responsibility of a conscious taste which knows how to select.

There is too much talk of how reading should be "guided" and readers "directed". These are dangerous terms which, in any case, have nothing to do with the true role of criticism, which is to bear witness rather than to teach. It cannot be held against a critic if he voices the aspirations and trends of a literary clique: minorities, and experimental minorities in particular, must be able to make themselves heard. But it is equally important for other critics to provide other evidence bringing larger groups of writers and readers into contact. This depends on their psychological and social personality, on their integration in the thought and the society of their times. The deeper and sturdier the roots that a critic sinks into his own time, the better equipped he is to speak for the countless anonymous readers with whom he has ties of every kind. The truer his independence as a writer and his freedom as a man, the more likely he is to provide the people at large with an accessible and intelligible image of literature.

This last point is important, for it relates to a new scale of criticism, opened up by such modern media of communication as films, radio, television and, to a certain extent, strip cartoons. Nowadays, the critic can speak to the general public on behalf of literature and can reach that public. He need do no more than become an adapter or commentator. A sensitive and straightforward analysis of a text is tremendously effective on the television screen. The interpretation of a literary masterpiece on television or radio may perhaps be a misconstruction of the work, but it is certainly of the type of those that we have called "creative treasons". Film producers have always encouraged people to see the film after reading the book. To read the book after seeing the film is no less to be recommended and in all probability more fruitful.

Good criticism consists in calling the muses down from on high to take their place among human beings. Here we have the same values of action, commitment and humanism which enable writers to break away from their solitude in the modern community. The critic can become a mediator and a witness only if he is first of all a militant. As Richard Altick has pointed out (6), the Methodist preacher who, in the nineteenth century, was the narrowest and most didactic of censors, had been one of the most effective popularizers of literature in the preceding century. It was John Wesley himself who, as early as 1743, published an abridged pocket edition of Bunyan's *Pilgrim's Progress* at fourpence. His successors were to follow this trend and circulate books which were by no means all religious, since they included some of the best romantic poetry, but which all crossed the social barrier on the same wave of faith and enthusiasm. Methodist preaching and the cultural work that accompanied it are among the real causes of the sudden literary advancement of the British people at large, of the resulting mutation of books, and of the new course taken by English literature from 1830 onwards. If, at that point, the influence of the religious movement proved deadening rather than stimulating for Victorian literature, it was because Methodism, like so many other movements, had by then begun to conceal the fact that its enthusiasm was dwindling under a mask of strict dogmatism.

It may be thought that such considerations have nothing to do with the problem of criticism. In fact, however, the situation of the critic in our paperback civilization may be compared to that of the wandering preacher going from village to village. He has his personal mission but this must be subordinate, on the one hand, to the message which is transmitted through him without being his, and, on the other, to the actual situation of the living communities which he has to penetrate without doing violence to their group consciousness or interfering with the expression of that consciousness, which is always a frail thing.

To put it more simply, this means that any literary criticism suited to mass-circulation literature should be based on a knowledge of the literary behaviour of the public at large, acquired from inside, and personal experience of it. In the extreme case, it may even be considered that the critic is not absolutely needed as an intermediary. In the socialist countries, contacts between writers and workers in various sectors are systematically organized, being based on living as a community and working as a team. These methods are undoubtedly effective, but it is difficult to do without an organizer to establish a common language and prevent misunderstandings. Here, perhaps, is the new figure needed in our present age—the cultural leader who does not restrict himself to the facile resources of image and sound but uses them in order to undertake, with all the intellectual humility and team spirit required, the difficult task of organizing communication between the people at large and the individual.

The success of mass-circulation literature depends on the existence of such exchanges. The meeting-ground will necessarily be non-literary precisely because the exchanges must go beyond the limits of the cultivated public. Even if a writer and a reader are physically and intellectually very distant from one another, the sharing of trade union, political, religious or even just sports activities may make it possible to create the conditions required for communication between them.

It is here that the literary prize, so often and unfairly denounced, may take on a fresh significance. Such attempts at making a responsible selection from a necessarily anarchic output are useful and even vital in themselves. They essentially imply an academy, for through them a representative selection of cultivated people belonging to a certain social group clearly and firmly express the preferences of that group. In various forms, the system operated very satisfactorily for centuries, in fact so long as the cultivated group remained relatively small and homogeneous. The difficulties began in the nineteenth century, and have steadily increased up to the present, as new social groups took their place in forming literary opinion, set up their own academic standards and developed their own judgments. One of the results of this increase in the number of academies, whether avowedly such or not, is the present plethora of literary prizes which deprives the selection of all its value.

But there is something still more serious to be considered. In an *élite* culture, values remain stable whereas, in a mass culture, they are fluid and constantly called in question, since what is involved is a way of life rather than a way of being. The academic accolade of the literary prize is, in the literal sense of the word, a consecration. It marks out the author as one entitled to the enduring respect of his peers for certain merit which can never again be depreciated, but it also places him irremediably out of reach of the people as a whole by transforming him into a celebrity. This phenomenon of celebrity, very clearly recognized by Carlyle as early as 1840 (7), dates from the earliest large-scale printings at the beginning of the nineteenth century. One of the most spectacular examples at that time was the Byron cult. By no means all the winners of the Prix Goncourt or the Nobel Prizes in our own day receive the hero-worship from which Byron suffered, which was almost comparable with that now extended towards film stars; but the mere prestige of their awards turns them, as it were, into institutions, legends, totems or, at best, shining examples. This is one of the swiftest forms of that literary death which accompanies success and, unless he has an exceptional determination to recreate himself and maintain his independence, no writer can hope to escape it.

With or without mass-circulation books, societies possessing a long-established literary tradition will find it difficult to preserve themselves from the academic reflex and will long continue to treat their writers as heroes of the mind, but the younger nations where literature is currently emerging must beware of the snare of institutionalization. If they set up literary prizes—and they would be wrong to disdain this method of selecting and encouraging writers—they will have to ensure that these reflect broad currents of opinion deriving from the inmost feelings of the people, even perhaps before the intellect comes into play at all. With all due respect, it may be asked whether those mysterious ground swells which lift up to the heights of glory this or that singer or musician, or even this or that poet who has chosen the record as his medium, may not be more effective and more authentic than the pondered judgments of the experts. The ideal would be for the two forms of evaluation to be in agreement, but this is still, for the time being, a vain hope.

Active readers and passive readers

We must, after all, face up to the facts. The present mutation in the world of books may prove successful but will be neither complete nor final. We may talk of mass circulation, but by no means all the "masses" are involved. Even in the most advanced countries, only a fraction of those able to read will take to reading during the present stage—that fraction which succeeds in gaining control of the social structures required for that end. In the developing countries—and we must bear in mind that the reading public in Asia represents a quarter of the total population and in Africa one-eighth—many other stages and many other mutations will be needed before whatever is to replace books as they now are (perhaps at no very distant date) can ensure that the messages of information and culture circulate freely among all men.

But even then there will still be active and passive readers. There will always be people who, through idleness, timidity or inclination, will decline communication with the writer. There will always be those who love books as objects and will not dissociate the message of the binder and the printer from that of the writer.

This is of no great importance. The main thing is to ensure that active readers should be more and more numerous and more and more receptive. There is no reason why plastic values should not be integrated with the values of action, intelligence and sensitivity—in fact, with all those values which give reading its place in human life. The revolution in publishing is the most liberal of all revolutions.

All it asks is that there be neither prejudice nor inflexibility. Fetishism or fanaticism attached to books is incompatible with the generosity of books. Books are like bread. Throughout the world, the production of grain and the basic foodstuff derived from it was primitive man's great victory over hunger. The result was that bread became something almost holy, the symbol of liberating labour, survival and communion. The instinctive reactions of many peoples still embody this sort of innate respect for bread, which is obscurely enshrined in their collective memory as a saviour. Books are the object of the same sort of unacknowledged veneration since they were the bread of the mind, the great victory achieved by somewhat less primitive men over ignorance and the slavery it means. A book which does not last, an ephemeral book, a book which is an act and not necessarily a lasting reality, a treasure to be preserved, a possession for all time—*ktêma es aeï*—is something which profoundly shocks our instinctive feelings and may even disgust us.

At the same time, we are very well aware that the poor man's bread in the present-day world has ceased to be a symbol and has become a mere metaphor, and a bad one at that. We know that the world's hunger will not be overcome this time by the individual magic of the ear or the loaf, but by a vast collective effort bringing into play all the scientific, technical, and mechanical resources of the advanced civilizations, by a profound and systematic reform of social structures, by a concerted world policy which will affect many other sectors besides those of agriculture and food.

Nor can the great hunger of the mind be overcome in any other way. The individual demands of writers, the refined tastes of cultivated book-lovers, should be given neither more nor less weight in our plans for the future than the majestic gesture of the sower or the gastronomy of Brillat-Savarin in the discussions of the Food and Agriculture Organization. We must deny nothing, but nor must we interpose anything between books and life, and especially not myths. We are living in an age when great things are being done by teams assisted by machines. We readily accept this for the arts which have developed along with mass civilization, such as radio, television and films, not to mention the theatre, where there is direct contact with the audience and where the principle has always been more or less accepted. We must now go on to accept it in respect of books. It goes without saying that the very nature of reading will always necessitate a greater measure of solitude than other forms of communication or artistic expression, but the solitude of the writer, like the solitude of the reader, is not anti-social. It is only the means whereby each may find the other. A man reading alone in his room often has more companions than if he were watching a film with a thousand other spectators in a cinema.

It is this inherent virtue of books which must be maintained and developed. Dissemination, limitless and ceaselessly renewed communication among all men—that is the true function of the book. Once it ceases to fulfil it, however fine its appearance and however noble its content, it is merely so much waste-paper, a soul-less treasure. One might as well put a stone in its place.

NOTES

(1) According to J. W. Saunders, *The Profession of English Letters*, Routledge and Kegan Paul, London, 1964, "The average reward for the good romantic novelist is somewhere in the region of £150 per novel" (p. 241). See also R. Escarpit, *La rentabilité de la littérature*, Actes de 5ᵉ Congèrs de la Société française de Littérature comparée, Lyon, 1962.

(2) As regards the problem of a second profession, see Taha Hussein's articles, *The Writer in the World Today*, in *The Artist in Modern Society* (International Conference of Artists, Venice, 22–28 September 1952), Paris, Unesco, 1954, pp. 69–83.

(3) André Thérive, *La foire littéraire*, Paris, La Table Ronde, 1963, p. 225.

(4) *Ibid.*

(5) *Ibid.*, p. 256.

(6) *The English Common Reader*, pp. 99–128.

(7) Thomas Carlyle, *On Heroes, Hero-Worship and the Heroic in History*, London, 1840, Lecture V, *The Hero as Man of Letters*.